THE TECHNICAL MANAGER'S SURVIVAL GUIDES

CHANGE MANAGEMENT

Concepts and Practice

By Marcus Goncalves

Other Titles in Series - The Technical Manager's Survival Guides
Vol. 1 *Team Building* by Marcus Goncalves (2006)
Vol. 2 *Managing Systems Development 101*, by James T. Karam (2007)

Library of Congress Cataloging-in-Publication Data

Goncalves, Marcus.
  Change management : concepts and practice / by Marcus Goncalves.
     p. cm.
  Includes index.
  ISBN 978-0-7918-0264-9
  1. Organizational change--Management. 2. Information technology--Management. 3. Knowledge management. I. Title.

  HD58.8.G66 2007
  658.4'06--dc22

                    2007028265

Preface

If we allow ourselves to reminisce back in history, to the time of kingdoms and wars for supremacy, we find that such wars were fought for survival and expansion. Monarchs, full of zest and vigor, were highly motivated towards achieving their goal but often their wars were primitive. Whoever updated their techniques and weaponry was the winner. The British domination of colonies was a case in point. The difference between winning and losing laid in the upgrading of operational techniques which, of course, was backed by strong motivation. In business, the story is very similar

A large corporation with talented human resources, but averse to change, fails and fails miserably, while small companies, with perfect foresight and flexibility towards change, succeed. No longer is the big swallowing the small, but it is the fast that is outpacing the slow. Business leaders, from Jack Welch and Bill Gates, owe their success to change management. If a corporate has to be evaluated in terms of success or failure it can be said in no unequivocal terms that it is the ability to manage change on the part of the business leader and his team down the line. It may be a good idea to evolve some quantitative measures of this quality of management apart from evaluating profitability and financial position.

Herein lays a role for professionals. One of the most important roles of a leader today is to put the business and market strategies in place and then influence and direct the business to ensure the goals and objectives are met. Trying to keep up with the constant pace of change makes this a tough challenge.

This book helps such leaders to focus their organization on a winning game plan and the process of change. It also should enable leaders with tools to forecast the future, balance organic growth, and put in place an effective strategic measurement system that provides a real-time method of perceiving organizational performance in the midst of change.

In *Change Management: Concepts and Practice*, you will hopefully understand that implementing changes in organizations is often easier said than done. The process requires not only a transfer of knowledge, but also the establishment of a different behavior. Thus, organizations should not only think about the technical aspects of implementation, such as the development of a new IT system to support the change, but also about whether people are still well placed in the organization, and whether they are sufficiently trained to handle the change. This requires considerable time and attention in a change process. My hope is that this book will provide you with an overview of what change management entails, its advantages (and necessity!), pitfalls to watch for during implementation, and some strategies and activities for becoming change agents.

This book is not, however, intended to comprehensively cover the subject. There are a lot of resources available out there and the bibliography may help you in expanding your knowledge on the topic. The idea of this book is to provide you with a good overview on the topic. The book also should serve as a resource companion for those professionals attempting the Engineering Management Certificate International (EMCI) offered by the American Society of Mechanical Engineers (ASME), for which this book was carefully tailored. But, of course, this book can be of great use to any business professionals seeking to develop an effective change management strategy.

The book is broken up into ten chapters covering all the main aspects of the change management process. Here it is an overview of the book:

Chapter 1, *The Need for Change Management*, provides you with an overview of the change management process and why today's business practices require organizations, whether large or small, commercial or industrial, to change their ways, fast and often.

Chapter 2, *Anticipating and Promoting Change*, provides an insight on the advantages of having an organization investing in change management by developing change agents capable of anticipating and planning for necessary changes.

Chapter 3, *Overcoming Emotional Obstacles*, conveys the importance of attending to emotional side of change, the one carried by the people being asked to change. Every time a process is changed people must change. This chapter discusses the emotional barrier that is often created in light of change and strategies to deal with it.

Chapter 4, *Planning Change*, shows how important it is to have a well thought out plan before engaging in any change process. It discusses the need for leadership support and the stages that the change process must go through.

Chapter 5, *Managing Change*, picks up where chapter 4 left by bringing a pragmatic approach to change management and discussing how vital it is to manage change and assess its earned value.

Chapter 6, *Dealing With Resistance to Change*, complements the discussion introduced in chapter 3, as it offers several strategies to dealing with people's resistance to change.

Chapter 7, *Embracing Change Management*, offers a discussion on how change management must be constant, a work in progress, an attitude an organization and its people must embody and embrace, rather than a finite process.

Chapter 8, *Using GE's Change Acceleration Process*, provides a brief overview of GE's acclaimed CM process and how it can assist your organization.

Chapter 9, *Using Kaizen in the Change Process*, introduces you to this Japanese change/improvement technique and how to use it to enhance your change management process. The chapter also provides some overview of Six Sigma and few other approaches to the change management process.

Chapter 10, *Becoming a Learning Organization: Ready for Change*, discusses how important it is for an organization to change its culture from a reactive one, to one that is learning-focused and a catalyst for change.

Who Should Read This Book

This book is primarily designed for those who are or plan to be involved with change management projects, as well as for anyone interested or immersed in such process; for project and team managers, project and team leaders or anyone performing in those roles or soon to be performing in those roles.

Acknowledgment

I have been thinking about this book for some time now. A lot of it is a result of my own consulting work, but many professionals in the industry, friends, co-workers and clients played a major role in it as well.

Aware of the fact that thanking everyone would be near to impossible, if I miss some of their names, please forgive me. I would like to start by thanking Mary Grace Stefanchik, the editor at the American Society of Mechanical Engineers (ASME), for not only inviting me to write another book for ASME's collection, but especially for her patience with me, my busy schedule, and the personal challenges I faced in 2006; to professor Vijay Kanabar, at Boston University for his great friendship, professionalism, and excellent insights in project and change management. I also would like to thank Newton Scavone, director of Human Resources at International Paper of Brazil, for his expert feedbacks prior to the conclusion of this book; professor Kip Becker, Ph.D., Chairman, Department of Administrative Sciences at Boston University; for his unconditional support, especially during 2006, with the passing of my children Joshua and Andrea.

I would also like to express my appreciation to many corporate leaders that shared their views and experiences with me about team building, project and operations management. My special thanks go to the following leaders: Kerri Apple, SVP at Corpus Incorporated; Larry Miller, at PPL Montana; James Willey, at Covanta Energy of the Philippines; Mark Payne, at International Paper in U.S.; and Michael Tinkleman, Ph.D., director of research at ASME in Washington, D.C. for all his support.

Many thanks also go to my spiritual leaders at the Boston Church of Christ, Ken Ostrowski and Mike Van Auken, for their continuous support and friendship. Last but not least, my deepest gratitude to my wife Carla, sons Samir and Josh (in memory), and my princess Andrea (also in memory), for their unconditional support during the many hours it took to write this book. I could not forget Ninigapa (in memory of Paganini, the previous bird), my parakeet, and Gus, the dog!

To God be the glory!

Dedication

To my forever beautiful wife Carla, my son and friend Samir, and especially, in memory of my princess and daughter Andrea, and my young prince Joshua, who passed away during the writing of this book. These are the real treasures of my life.

To God be the glory.

Marcus Goncalves

Table of Contents

Chapter 1
The Need for Change Management

Executive sponsors often fail to personally engage as the sponsor for the change.

As corporations migrate to a knowledge-centric operation, positioning, planning, leadership, board and executive management support all become crucial. However, change management (CM) most often is not easily plugged into an ROI (return of investment) equation. In addition, these first few years of the twenty-first century have been characterized by an economic downturn not seen since the information-driven economy emerged in the early 1990s, shifting the focus of executive performance to be measured no longer by results only, but by goals as well.

Until recently, the business-critical value of change management investment was all but assumed, and experts on the subject all realized their old assumptions were wrong. Many predicted, and are still predicting, that change management and its derived career paths are doomed to extinction. In fact, during the spring of 2001, CIO magazine commented that change management systems didn't work, in particular due to the fact that no one in the organization would use or support such systems, beginning with upper management. And they were right!

The theory that change management systems (and let's include knowledge management as well) are only as good as their information technology (IT) has been nearly unquestionable. But I believe the thinking behind this theory is murky. You see, as the first generation of MIS professionals grew up from accounting and financial departments, their efforts were focused on enhancing accounting and financial practices. Similarly, the first breed of change management professionals grew up from information technology, information systems and management; hence their practices have been heavily focused on systems and technology. That is precisely why most change management problems occur.

As companies focus on building knowledge database repositories and data mining techniques, a lot of change is introduced. Every time a process is changed, workers must change as well. The majority of workers, however, are ignored, and so are their cultural issues. In addition, I believe the massive investments in knowledge management projects in the 1990's were meant to underlie the historical globalization, merger and acquisition (M&A) activities across the globe that characterized that decade.

Technology became one of the most active M&A sectors during the late 1990's, as figure 1.1 shows[1]. Consequently, the need for information sharing among disparate systems and knowledge bases was too great. Even though the objective evidence for such a claim is controversial at best, change management has had a free ride for at least the last three or four years.

Figure 1.1 – Technology became the most active M&A sector during the late 1990's.

The Era of Change Management Accountability

Well, the ride is over. The era of change management accountability has come, and corporate change management systems will be judged on the basis of their ability to deliver a quantifiable competitive advantage, capable of making businesses smarter, faster, and more profitable. In the process, the need to sell the change management concept to employees shouldn't be underestimated. In a fast-paced global economy, executives and chief knowledge officers (CKO's) should strive to promote an environment where an individual's knowledge is valued and rewarded, and a changing process is established, promoting a culture that recognizes tacit knowledge and encourages every one to share it in the process of change. How we go about it is the challenge.

The old practice of employees being asked to surrender their will and experience, and just change when they are asked to, threatens the very traits that make them valuable as individuals. That attitude must change. Change cannot be forced; if so, it dies and gives birth to bitterness and resentment, and that is very bad for business! That is why motivating employees to contribute to change management activities through implementation of incentive programs is frequently ineffective. Often, employees tend to participate in such programs solely to earn incentives, without regard to the quality or relevance of the changes they adopt or contribute to.

The main challenge here is that CM is overwhelmingly a cultural undertaking. Before setting the course for a CM project and deciding on CM practices, you will have to know what kinds of changes your organization's employees need to undertake, and what techniques and practices should be implemented to get them through it. Thus you will need a change management strategy that reflects and serves a business' goals and attributes. A dispersed, global organization, for example, is probably not well-served by a highly centralized change management strategy.

To be successful, professionals involved in change management processes must become change agents themselves. They must be able to implement a very transparent change management activity, one that is focused on simplicity and common sense, and is at no time imposed. Whatever is imposed will always be opposed, which immediately compromises the value and integrity of the change process. Ideally, participation in change management efforts should be desired by every employee, should come from within, and should be its own reward. After all, the goal of such initiatives should be to make life easier for employees, therefore positively affecting the bottom line. Otherwise, such effort has failed.

---

[1] According to SG Cowen, source: SDC. Note, the percent value represents the technology M&A activity in comparison to the total M&A activity

Technology Became the Most Active M&A Sector During the Late 1990's

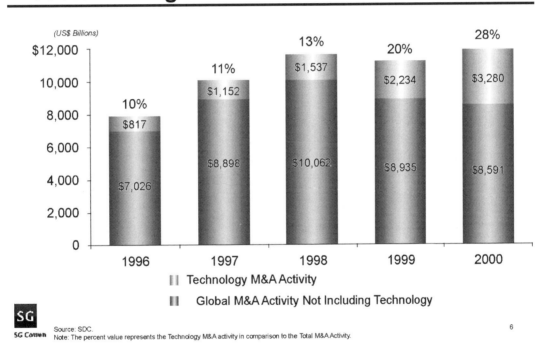

Figure 1.1

Unfortunately, the majority of CM projects to date have not achieved the level of success expected. The lack of transparent integration between IT and other technical groups, and CM tools and the users often have them thinking CKOs and CM agents don't know what they are doing. Thus, today's CM agents must be able to successfully leverage the promise of CM, its perils and, in many instances, eye-popping costs in infrastructure, deployment, implementation, and use of the system.

No doubt CM can revolutionize a corporation's ability to adapt to new market trends and business requirements. But it won't be easy, and not likely cheap, as the challenges are many, and breaking down users' resistance is one of the major challenges change agents face. You don't get moving just by adopting and implementing one of the many CM toolkits and practices available on the market. My advice is for you to spend quality time planning your CM strategy, and be forewarned that the initiative may be expensive, not only in terms of capital investment, but also human, resource and organizational investments. With this in mind, you will be able to better plan for it. You should begin with the challenges discussed here. Then you should focus on the many strategies outlined throughout this book, which affect not only an organization's support, but also cultural and business issues, and ultimately the role of the CM agent (or the CKO) as catalyst and flagship for the whole process.

Defining Success in CM Implementations: Vision in Action

The ultimate goal of a CKO should be to bridge the gap between a corporation's know-how and its need-to-know. Even if a CM implementation is successful from the technical, usability, knowledge aggregation and retrieval viewpoints, empowering the organization to transform its know-how into how-to is still virtually a utopist task. But I'm a believer that the definition of success is *vision in action*. Seeking business success, several companies undertake tremendous reengineering cycles, and hire expensive management and business consultants who, after generating reports and more reports, tell them what they often already know, and have know for years.

You might have a clear vision of your CM project goals, but if you don't have a clear action plan in place, one that can be measured using reliable metrics, you just won't succeed. By the same token, you may have a clear action plan, one that very likely has been outlined, developed and recommended in-house or by outside consultants, but if you don't have a clear vision of where you are going, the results you want to achieve, you just won't get there either.

Don't underestimate the complexity of CM implementations. If you look at enterprise resource planning (ERP) and customer relationship management (CRM) solutions you have some idea. Very, but very few ERP implementations have been fully successful; most of them are still in the implementation phase, being clogged up with CRM solutions, or already undergoing some level of business process rethinking. The same goes for CRM. According to Meta Group's March 2000 survey, 55 to 75 percent of CRM projects do not meet their objectives. Further, according to Insight Technology Group, more than 25 percent of 226 CRM users surveyed do not think the implementation will add any significant improvement in company operations, and only 50 percent think there will be some sort of improvement. Now, CRM success results are much more tangible to measure than CM ones!

What those surveys underline is an increasing skepticism about intelligent systems. CKO's and change agents must be able to avoid, if not eliminate them. To get 100 percent satisfaction in CM implementations is not only very expensive, but near to impossible. It's not enough to announce a CM strategy. You need to convince your people to change, and it should start with upper management.

The Challenge of Defining Specific CM Goals

Since the late 1990s CM has been emerging as a preeminent articulation of post-modern, post-industrial innovational management theory, increasingly adopted by corporations and governments. However, defining specific CM goals have never been harder.

While hyper proponents of CM see it as the ultimate new age management construction, so vital that yesterday is too late to start a program, and so intangible that no one can agree on what it is, there has always been confusion about the term "change management" itself. It has been used in information systems, strategy meetings and many other business disciplines without any consistency. Often you find the term used in trade magazines, by technologists, financial analysts and even sociologists, all in their own context. Unfortunately, there is no clear agreement on what CM is, which makes the definition of specific CM goals even more difficult.

A CM program should always be in tune with business goals, and no matter what CM goals are, there must be an underlying business reason to do so. Otherwise, CM is a futile venture. To gauge the degree of alignment of a CM program with business goals, utilize the following pointers:

- Does your CM program address the strategic notion of organizational survival and competence within a fundamentally changing and unpredictable organizational environment?

- Does your CM go beyond traditional business management needs?

- Does your CM take into consideration the human-centric notion of knowledge, in relationship to the professional activity context of the organization, as well as the lack of it, which will define levels of performance?

- Does it provide for incorporation of the creative capabilities of people, necessary for innovative breakthroughs with the optimization-based, efficiency enhancement capabilities of advanced new strategies?

When defining specific CM goals, change agents must keep in mind that such programs are not static, as the value (and need) of change can grind down over time. To prevent change from getting stale too fast, CM program contents should be periodically updated, amended and even discarded when necessary.

Innovation will address the relevance of change, as it is prone to subsequent changes at any given time, often as a result or catalyst of employee skills set changes. Therefore, there is no endpoint to a CM program. Like product development, marketing and R&D, CM is a constantly evolving business practice.

The Challenge of *Intrapreneurship*

One of the major challenges change agents are facing in this fast-paced, Internet-based, global economy is the redefinition of employment contracts in U.S. and other worldwide organizations. This is because, in such environments, the need for change in the organizational business process becomes increasingly relevant, forcing employees of knowledge-based organizations to act as knowledge intrapreneurs[2].

In order to compete in a timely manner, intrapreneurship is a must, as the nature of organizations and work roles are changing, and must continue to change! In such an environment, emerging work roles must rely on and exploit an *informated*[3] environment by making the information base of the organization available to members at all levels, assuring that each has the knowledge, skills and authority (yes, authority!) to engage with the change productively. An efficient operation in the informed workplace requires a more equitable change process and authority. Such changes require new work roles of every employee, roles that call them to become an extension of their managers, as well as an intrapreneur in the organizational knowledge-creation process.

The knowledge intrapreneurs should be expected to contribute to organizational knowledge-creation processes, based on developing knowledge relationships and knowledge exchanges within and outside the formal boundaries of the organization. As a result, a new and emerging virtual community of practice and virtual events within and outside the organization will take place, at global levels, harbingering this vision.

The Challenge of Delivering Tangible Benefits with CM

In today's event and information-driven economy, companies are discovering that most opportunities, and ultimately value, are derived from intellectual rather than physical assets. To get the most value from a company's intellectual assets, CM professionals are striving to share knowledge throughout the organization, its partners, supply chain and distribution channels, serving as a foundation for collaboration.

Yet to have CM programs deliver better collaboration is not an end in itself, and does not necessarily provide tangible benefits to the organization. In fact, it may even increase the level of complexity of the information systems already in place, impairing knowledge sharing and causing a burst of information overflow, often out of context. And without an overarching business context, CM is meaningless at best and harmful at worst. Thus, the new breed of change agents must follow the words of the strategist Gary Hamel, when he says that "wealth creators change the rules." [4] This new breed of change agents must become rule makers, and in the process, they must break a few CM rules as well.

---

[2] Such a concept is actually not new, as Dr. Yogesh Malhotra, the founding chairman and chief knowledge architect of the BRINT Institute, had pointed it out back in 1998 on a change management discussion forum at Brint (www.brint.com)

[3] As termed by Dr. Malhotra (see previous footnote).

[4] In "Leading the Revolution," Harvard Business School, August 2000

Making sense of information is a very important process in CM, not only because it can be a catalyst in bridging the gap between know-how and how-to, but it provides the only way I trust in allowing CM to be successfully measured: by directly impacting the bottom-line in a positive way, by generating savings, if not competitive advantage. Of course, there are other measurable benefits CM can provide, but those are typically more difficult to quantify.

In addition to delivering tangible results, an effective CM program should help an organization to:

- Foster innovation by inspiring the free flow of ideas

- Increase revenues by getting products and services to market faster

- Streamline operations and reduce costs by eliminating redundant or unnecessary processes

In the words of Kathy Harris, vice president and research area director at Gartner[5], "CM benefits are best achieved when linked to a specific business initiative that clearly provides specific benefits or value to the business." The ability to change is the link, or the terrain, your company (and your competition!) relies on to build a successful business. It is the battlefield where the new economy is taking place. As contenders in this digital Darwinism, corporations must take advantage of the terrain, their change management strategy, to advance.

To be successful in managing this process, or terrain, you must control scattering terrain, generated by economic shifts, new trends, M&A activity and so on, by not fighting it. Rather, you must embrace it! Sun Tzu's ideas about types of terrain, in The Art of War[6], define this principle very well. Here it is what he says about controlling terrain[7]:

> **Control easy terrain by not stopping**
>
> **Control disputed terrain by not attacking**
>
> **Control open terrain by staying with the enemy's force**
>
> **Control intersecting terrain by uniting with your allies**
>
> **Control dangerous terrain by plundering**
>
> **Control bad terrain by keeping on the move**
>
> **Control confined terrain by using surprise**
>
> **Control deadly terrain by fighting**

Therefore, a creative approach to CM can result in improved efficiency, higher productivity and increased revenues in practically any business function. Lessons learned can save you a lot of money and time. In addition, documenting best practices, success stories and lessons learned is an important component of the CM strategy.

---

[5] CIO Magazine, "Strategic Directions: Change management & e-Learning," in the article "Transforming the Way Organizations Work, June 2001
[6] Oxford University, 1984.
[7] Make sure to replace the word "terrain" with "knowledge" and you should have a powerful strategy for CM

The Challenge of Leading a CM Program

Historically, CM has been always characterized as the process through which organizations generate value from their change process and business realignment. Typically, generating value from such assets involves sharing them among employees, departments, and even with other companies in an effort to devise best CM practices.

Therefore, if we agree that CM is a business practice, and not a technology-based concept, CM programs should be lead by the CKO, or whoever is the change agent, and not the chief information officer (CIO). Of course, CIOs might be the most indicated professional, if the CM implementation is contained within the IT department, with very specific deliverables and expectations. Nonetheless, although it may appear to be obvious that CM programs should be lead by CKOs/change agents, many companies have dedicated CM staff headed by CIOs, CTOs, and other high-profile executives.

The problem with using CIOs and CTOs to lead CM projects is that typically these professionals tend to approach CM programs from the technology point of view, relying on IT. But such reliance to promote corporate competitive advantage no longer provides guaranteed successful results, as the business world has become so volatile that the same change process in a certain time and context can be totally irrelevant, if not incorrect in another time and context. Thus one of the main challenges in leading CM programs concerns the value of the change process being implemented, as not all change is valuable.

Change management processes tend to either be explicit or tacit, as found in knowledge managemen. Explicit change, the type that is documented, required and codified, though laborious, is generally manageable. But a much harder concept to grasp is the tacit change, the one that takes place in people's heads. The challenge inherent with tacit change is figuring out how to recognize, generate, share and manage it. While IT in the form of e-mail, groupware, instant messaging and related technologies can help facilitate the dissemination of tacit change, identifying such change in the first place is very often a major challenge.

In addition, change agents must be able to bring every department, every individual on board with the CM program. Executives, as well as other high-level staff and decision-makers, must be sold on the program. Make sure to have a list of very tangible and quantifiable benefits and results CM will bring. If possible, try to map out the increase in revenues the company can expect from an improved CM process.

Then you should get ready to persuade the rest of the organization. One alternative is to outsource the task. Hiring a consulting firm to spend time educating, setting expectations and listening to concerns expressed by company's employees before the CM system goes live is advisable. By explaining how the new CM system would make their job simpler and less complex, you increase the chances of receiving full support from the company as a whole, which will be vital for the success of your project.

Once you have convinced employees that CM is good for business, and for them, it is time to retrain them: change begins. CM systems change the way people work. Unless you educate them about such impact and how to use and take advantage of the new system, your project may go awry and people will not support it. Best practices indicate that for every dollar spent on CM systems you will have to spend at least another dollar and a half on awareness and training programs.

Be prepared to find resistance, as people tend to be very uneasy about sharing their knowledge and best practices in lieu of change, for fear of becoming a dispensable commodity inside the organization.

The Challenge of Managing Change

Change management above all is a business strategy, and as such it has the potential to fundamentally change the behavior of any organization. CM is so fundamental that it requires calibrated strategies and tactics in every core business function. Thus, one of the main challenges in managing change is to gain full support from the executive staff. If the CEO and the executive management team are not supportive of the CM strategy, rest assured there is no chance CM can play a major role in transforming your organization.

However, many corporations are not yet clear about the need to manage change. In 2003, the Conference Board surveyed 158 companies on the subject and found that 80 percent had launched some kind of CM activity, but only 15 percent had specific, stated CM objectives and goals.

As organizations begin to rely more and more on CM programs, CM professionals must realize that mere policies and procedures cannot hope to provide all levels of change today's organizations require. Any fundamental change within the organization requires the generation and effective deployment of a culture that embraces change and the need for change. Knowledge such as how to penetrate and dominate global and new markets, enhancement of employee recruitment and retention, and better and more rapid development of products and services, must be cataloged, aggregated, and managed in order to aid change processes.

To be effective, especially in challenging times, change management must encompass a structured system, with processes and technologies that inspire people to share what they know and use what they learn. This process should involve:

- Aiding and abetting collaboration, knowledge sharing and continual learning.

- Capturing the patterns recognized in human experience and insight (knowledge), and making them available to and reusable by others.

- Improving decision-making processes and quality.

- Making it easy to find and reuse this knowledge, either as explicit knowledge that has been recorded in physical form or as timely access to a human expert's tacit, intuitive knowledge.

Measuring Results

At the core of the success of any CM initiative is a premise that I believe every professional serious about his career should have. Instead of buying into the concept that you, a professional or a business, should know what you know and then profit from it, you should strive everyday to obsolete what you know before others obsolete it, and profit by creating the challenges and opportunities others haven't even thought about.

9

Such a premise may go against the leading business strategist authors and consultants out there, but I know for a fact that it works, and you need only ask any successful foreign immigrant in this country to confirm it. When I arrived in this country in 1986, I strived to obsolete myself as a burger maker at Burger King. With the grace of the almighty, working at the core of the city of Boston on Summer Street, I tried hard to obsolete myself, and I figured out a way to make 12 burgers in less than one minute. By doing so, I obsolescing my peer's way of doing burgers, and in the process I set a new standard for making burgers, got a medal and diploma from Burger King University and advanced myself to kitchen manager, all in less than three months on the job (and barely speaking English).

Another example is Ram Charan[8], who from his childhood in India, where he worked in his family's shoe shop, was able to break the rules by obsolescing himself and innovating. While attending Harvard Business School he reversed the rules of business and instituted the universal laws of business success, all based on common sense.

To remain competitive in the 21st century corporations must employ all the knowledge they can master to promote precise and timely change. By not sharing this knowledge with other corporations, such companies retain a unique advantage. However, unshared knowledge does not equal success if the knowledge is not shared within the organization and effectively quantified. Beware that intellectual property rights cannot do much to protect corporate knowledge. Only learning, which creates new knowledge, provides the primary competitive advantage, and radically impacts the organization.

As you think about how to measure the success of your CM implementation, consider the following indicators, and then plan and execute a clear strategy to address these problems at their source:

- What change management aspects do you need to manage in your organization? – Concentrate on real business needs, such as reduction of asset intensity and improvement of revenue collection.

- What are the high-transaction and short-cycle processes you must concentrate on? – Some key processes you should concentrate on includes accounts payable, customer service or inside sales, where the impact of your efforts will quickly be exposed.

- How important it is for you to include a review of your current business practices? – Watch for operations in which an ability to capture and reuse knowledge will improve efficiency, lower costs and boost profits.

- Are there any knowledge gaps, and if so, do you know why? – Make sure to identify any knowledge gaps and their origins, and try to determine if they are related to systems (IT), processes (management) or people (organization). Figure 1.2 depicts the relationships between information systems components. Knowledge gaps tend to be present in the unstructured nature of important decisions and diversity of managerial roles, and are often the cause for complexity in decision-making.

---

[8] Ram Charan is an adviser on corporate governance, CEO succession, and strategy implementation. He was named as Best Teacher by Northwestern's Kellogg School and as a top-rated executive educator by *Business Week*. He is author of *Boards at Work*, coauthor of *Every Business Is a Growth Business*, and a frequent contributor to *Harvard Business Review*. (6/2000)

Figure 1.2 – Process flow of information system models

- Is your CM implementation working accordingly? – In such a cognitive model, knowledge exists in context, making it difficult to measure success or failure, as results are not tangible but indirect. Therefore, you will be able to identify the results by measuring the impact of new tools and practices on your business, benchmarking its performance both before and after changes are being implemented.

- How can you consistently improve knowledge sharing? - Whether intended or not, most organizations reward those who hoard knowledge. Every knowledge-based organization has resident experts who revel in the status their knowledge brings them. Unfortunately, knowledge hoarding leads to reinventing the wheel. In addition, it often causes ill-informed decisions to be made, and the incurrence of unnecessary costs and revenue loss. Thus make sure to implement incentives that encourage employees to share knowledge and discourage hoarding. Figure 1.3 provides an outline of a typical knowledge-based organization. The challenge is to transform tacit knowledge into explicit, to make the transition from know-how to how-to.

Figure 1.3 – Knowledge-base view of firm

CM should be able to provide everyone within the organization with the tools that will enable them to obsolete themselves daily. CM tools should also empower workers to renew themselves daily as well. Measuring results is key in this process, as productive knowledge work should be very tangible, all about how each other's time and attention is used, as the people in the organization try to get their work done. Keep in mind that when it comes to CM, your worse challenge is day-to-day confusion or lack of clear key result areas. Thus, to survive and succeed, CM initiatives should bring about very tangible results, which should at least include:

- Reduction of product development times – Through CM programs Roche products are sent to FDA approval six months faster.

- Creation of more opportunities for innovation – CM enabled Dow Chemical to save $40 million a year through reuse of patents.

- Improvement of customer relationships – Ford Motor Co. saved more than $600 million over three years

- Ability to make decisions faster and closer to the point of action – Royal/Dutch Shell's deployment of a best-practice sharing methodology from Ford Motor Co. in two pilot

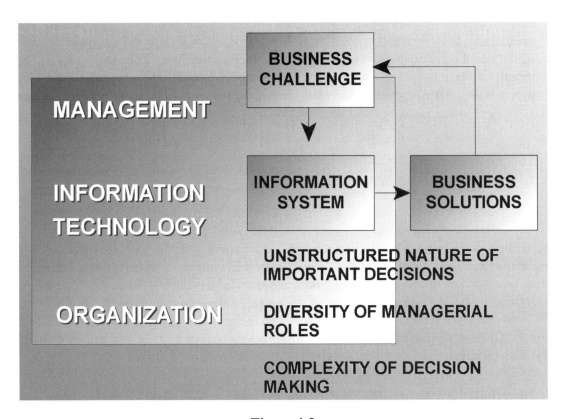

Figure 1.2

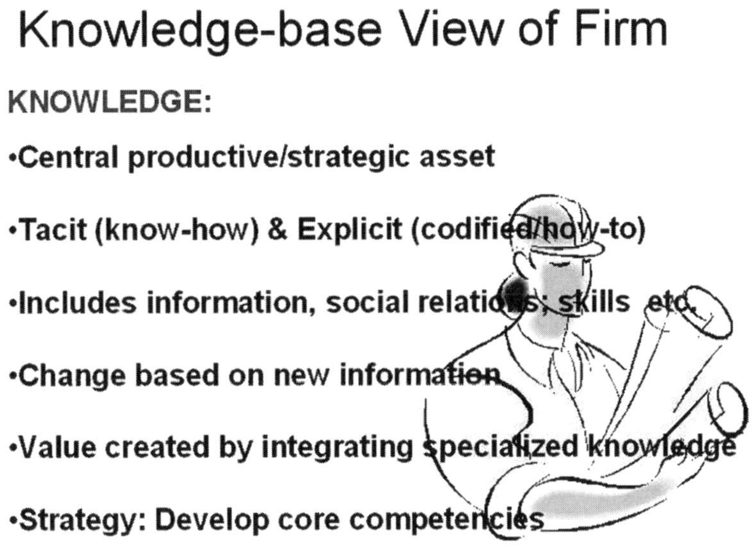

Knowledge-base View of Firm

KNOWLEDGE:

•**Central productive/strategic asset**

•**Tacit (know-how) & Explicit (codified/how-to)**

•**Includes information, social relations, skills etc.**

•**Change based on new information**

•**Value created by integrating specialized knowledge**

•**Strategy: Develop core competencies**

Figure 1.3

communities of practice realized cost avoidance and savings of more than $5 million in four months.

While many authors, specialized publications and corporate executives point out the failures of CM, the facts above shows that a well defined CM project can save an organization millions of dollars, a dramatic impact on the bottom-line. Thus today's change agents must be aware of the diversity of perspectives from which one can comprehend the concept of knowledge. In addition, be aware of problems with the generally known understandings and notions of management (in CM) that have filled many mainstream business texts, with regards to the value of CM.

Addressing the Challenges

Change management is without a doubt an oxymoron, which explains the difficulty in reconciling the soft issues around it, such as innovation and creativity, with hard issues, such as performance benchmarks measurement and assessment. There is a diametrically opposed assumption about the definition of, and nature between, change and management. Although CKOs and change agents tend to understand that management and control are not synonymous, this is not so for CTOs or CIOs which rely on controlling systems as a way of management.

The gap is based on the fact that the job descriptions of CIOs and CTOs, although a fairly new breed of professionals, have their roots in contemporary management theories, typically developed between 1930 and 1962. During this period, driven by social psychologists, organizational behaviorists and sociologists, the focus of management was to emphasize individual collective behavior. As discussed earlier in this chapter, the great majority of today's CKO's and change agents came from that era or were influenced by it. Many of them were former CIOs or CTOs, or adopted that management theory.

However, today's CKOs and change agents must fundament themselves in a post-modern theory of management, which began to gain ground after 1965. Actually, today's CKOs and change agents must transcend this post-modern management model to one that takes into consideration the fast changing business landscape, the roaming nature of professionals. I would call this new management theory a post-Internet one.

As a result of this super fast-paced business landscape, CM initiatives are often disappointing, as there is a lack of user uptake and a failure to integrate CM into everyday working practices. However, such outcomes can be avoided, and this is what this book is all about. For now, just keep in mind these best business practices:

- Make sure to tighten your CM efforts to high-priority business objective – As you wouldn't fish on a pond with a bazooka, don't invest on CM just for CM's sake. To be successful, change and learning goals must be articulated at the same level of an organization's business objectives. This is the only way learning and knowledge sharing can truly become culturally embedded in the organization.

- If you want CM to succeed, you must integrate your people with the organization's business process and the tool you will be using – CM should always be a work-in-progress, never a finite project. Its never-ending integrated process should always be the implementation of a competitive strategy which appreciates that learning and sharing knowledge are equally important.

- When considering starting a CM implementation, the best tools I can recommend are actually the cheapest in the whole process: pencil and paper. Make sure to have a knowledge strategy aligned with your organization's business strategy way before considering any technology tool. Make sure the strategy defines all key CM processes:

    a. Creation of strategies

    b. Identification of goals

    c. Development of the process

    d. Implementation mapping

    e. Knowledge sharing, application and reuse of it

FOOTNOTES

1) According to SG Cowen, source: SDC. Note, the percent value represents the technology M&A activity in comparison to the total M&A activity

2) The party relied on RetrievalWare search and retrieval software from the Viennese company Convera (www.convera.com)

3) Such concept is actually not new, as Dr. Yogesh Malhotra, the founding chairman and chief knowledge architect of the BRINT Institute had pointed it out back in 1998 on a change management discussion forum at Brint (www.brint.com)

4) As termed by Dr. Malhotra

5) Make sure to replace the word "terrain" with "knowledge" and you should have a powerful strategy for CM

6) Ram Charan is an adviser on corporate governance, CEO succession, and strategy implementation. He was named as Best Teacher by Northwestern's Kellogg School and as a top-rated executive educator by Business Week. He is author of *Boards at Work*[9], coauthor of *Every Business Is a Growth Business*[10], and a frequent contributor to Harvard Business Review.

---

[9] Jossey-Bass, 1998
[10] Times Books, 2000

Chapter 2
Anticipating and Promoting Change

Change before you have to.[1]

The title of this chapter was inspired by Spencer Johnson M.D.'s[2] acclaimed book *Who Moved my Cheese*. The book tells a simple and amusing story of four characters that live in a *maze* and look for *cheese*, a metaphor for what you want to have in life, to nourish them and make them happy. The story reveals profound truths about change that give people and organizations a quick and easy way to succeed in changing times.

In the story, two mice named Sniff and Scurry, and two people the size of mice, Hem and Haw, all of whom look and act a lot like regular people, are the protagonists. In the context of the story, *cheese* can be a good job, a loving relationship, money, a possession, health, or spiritual peace of mind, while the *maze* can be depicted as where you look for what you want, such as the organization you work in, or the family or community you live in.

In the story, the characters are faced with unexpected change. Eventually, one of them deals with change successfully, and writes what he has learned from his experience on the maze walls. When you come to see *The Handwriting on the Wall* you can discover for yourself how to deal with change, so that you can enjoy more success and less stress (however you define it) in your work and in your life.

Unfortunately, innovation has always been a primary challenge of leadership. Today we live in an era of such rapid change and evolution that leaders must work constantly to develop the capacity for continuous change and frequent adaptation, while ensuring that identity and values remain constant. They must recognize people's innate capacity to adapt and create -- to innovate.

The 21st century promises to be an exciting time. While there are many management, leadership and economic theories on what the future holds, we can all agree there will be a great deal of constant and revolving changes. Leaders must be prepared to successfully guide their groups and organizations through change to survive, innovate and prosper. This preparation should first begin with an

---

[1] Jack Welch, former CEO of GE
[2] http://www.whomovedmycheese.com

understanding of organizational culture and the levels of culture. Analyzing a group's artifact, values and beliefs, and basic assumptions will shed insight into the actions and reactions of that group.

Figure 2.1 - The 21st century promises to be an exciting time, with a great deal of constant and revolving changes. Successful innovators will be those able to bridge the knowledge gap between know-how and how-to implement change.

Leaders, in particular the executive staff, should understand that they are the most important players in the organizational change process. Using culture, creating or imbedding mechanisms, especially what users are interested in, sets the tone for the organization. Thus to be most effective, leaders must consistently act in ways that reinforce their values and the desired end state.

Through a human perspective, leaders can look at how to best match people's needs and skills with organizational goals. Power and competition for scare resources give a view from the political frame of reference. Finally, a symbolic frame of reference sheds light on a group's culture, including symbols, rituals, ceremonies, legends, heroes, and myths.

Change should not be seen as disruptive or threatening, as it provides new opportunity and resources for organizations to improve themselves through their own creative initiative, by generating innovation. It will take continued leadership effort and attention at all levels to complete the job, and leaders must be completely committed to creating an environment of trust, teamwork, and continuous improvement. It is only then that the organization will be an enterprise that allows each of its employees to achieve their full, God-given potential.

To thrive in the knowledge economy, organizations must continually renew their competitive strengths. Dorothy Leonard-Barton[3], a consultant specializing in innovation and a professor at the Harvard Business School, argues that "every *core capability* that leads to success is also *core rigidity*, and strengths can quickly become weaknesses." According to Leonard-Barton, organizations must consciously invest in activities such as collaboration, experimentation, prototyping and the acquisition of technological knowledge from outside the firm. She also adds that *if all employees conceive of their organization as a knowledge institution and care about nurturing it, they will continuously contribute to the capabilities that sustain it.*

Anticipating and Promoting Change

While everyone would agree that the 21st century holds many unknowns, to effectively manage any organization managers must realize that the knowledge economy is characterized by vast and dynamic changes. New technologies, in particular the Internet and knowledge technologies, as well as new regulations, directives, and resource restrictions, will be catalysts of change. But why do I believe CKOs and change agents are one of the most indicated leaders to hold the flag of organizational change, you

---

[3] In Wellsprings of Knowledge, Harvard Business School Press, 2000.

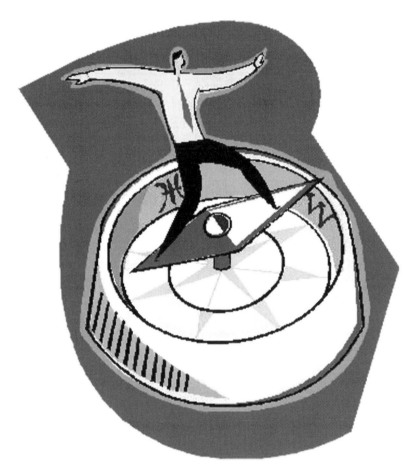

Figure 2.1

might ask? And what can CKOs and change agents do to prepare for, and successfully implement, effective and lasting organizational change?

Strategy in itself is a powerful tool in bringing clarity to any organization, as it can help integrate and focus energy, efforts, and resources. The reason I emphasize charting CKOs to lead change in organizations is because these professionals can take advantage of knowledge strategies, and can bring together three other critical leaders in the organization as members of the changing management process: the CTO or head of IT, the COO or head of HR, and the CEO. By bringing these leaders together, who rarely ever sit at a strategic table with each other (except for staff meetings), organizations are able to derive an integrated, focused, strategic force to their efforts.

The optimal structure of any corporate effort in change management will vary enormously according to the size of the organization, the degree of change, and the challenges it faces. One concern leaders have in charting CKOs and change agents with change management projects is the fear that new bureaucracies may be created. Thus to be successful in this endeavor, CKOs must not add any more red tape to an organization attempting to morph itself into something new, as business processes will definitely be affected by the changes, impacting policies and procedures, and consequently the existing bureaucracy. Change Management is the structured methodology for integrating change and the ability to adapt it throughout an organization. It is an organized, systematic application of the knowledge, tools, and resources of change to provide organizations with a key process to achieve their business strategy. As such, it is important to understand the forces that shape an organization's competitiveness, as depicted in Figure 2.2.

Figure 2.2 - The optimal structure in change management will vary enormously according to the size of the organization, the degree of change and the challenges it faces.

In addition, CKOs must posses excellent entrepreneurial traits, and be influential and persuasive enough to meet the knowledge economy's business challenges. That's why I emphasize in chapters one and two the urgent need of a new breed of CKO, more business-oriented, more focused on the bottom line of the business and not so much on data mining and warehousing, database marketing, or even e-commerce. These activities, with advanced software applications and business intelligence tools, are best taken care of by IT professionals and the CTO/CIO (with the cooperation of the CKO, of course).

Therefore, as opposed to launching corporate-wide knowledge initiatives without clear business objectives at the outset, one of the main roles best tailored to CKOs under change management is to first identify the business competencies that can be enhanced by KM. A key factor to be considered in this regard is that organizations develop different knowledge strategies depending on whether they are competing on cost, product innovation, customer relationship management (CRM), partner relationship management (PRM) or even supplier relationship management (SRM).

Another key challenge CKOs are better equipped to address is the need for systems that integrate knowledge, technology and people. Such concerns have been pointed out by Jim Bair, research director with the Gartner Group, who comments that we now have technologies at our fingertips, particularly the Web, that promise to enhance access to information and make it more pervasive and ubiquitous. Bair

19

Managing Organizational Change:
Forecast That Shape Organizational Competitiveness

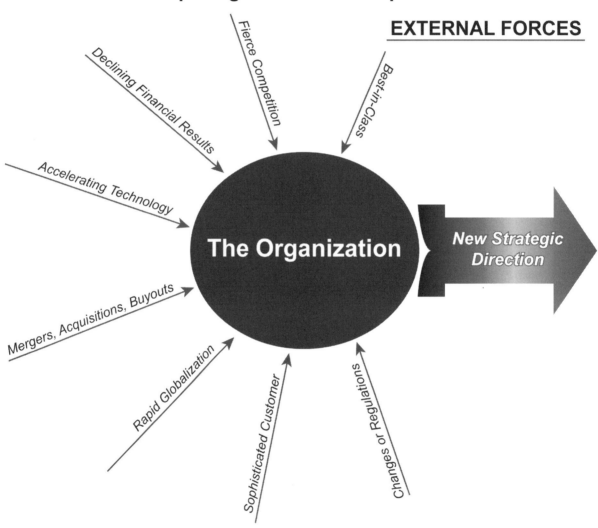

Figure 2.2

argues that organizations must now incorporate people into their KM efforts, and also contends that firms should place more emphasis on capturing the knowledge and expertise of their employees, and then ensuring it is effectively shared. *It is the uncaptured, tacit expertise and experience of employees that will make a big difference[4]*, he adds.

Bair's opinions notwithstanding, any organizational theory research will tell us that to change, an organization's leaders must first understand how an organization operates. This also requires an understanding of the organization's culture, how it was developed, and how it was analyzed. Furthermore, leaders must be able to view their organization from several points of view and perspectives to understand how it really functions. CKOs can play a major role in this process by helping leaders to unfreeze, restructure and refreeze their organization's culture as necessary. Or, if you prefer, remove, reshape and reposition the cheese inside their organization as necessary, in order to promote innovation.

I believe CKOs are the most indicated professionals to help in moving the cheese because of their exposure to knowledge management techniques, knowledge technologies, and the generators of knowledge: people, the Sniffs and Scurrys, Rams and Raws of every organization. This is a time-consuming process which requires a great deal of effort and consistency. Often senior management, in particular CTOs and CIOs, underestimate and misunderstand it, trying to address such cultural issues with Total Quality Management (TQM) implementations which can be very expensive, lengthy and ineffective. The United States Air Force, for instance, overestimated their TQM implementation and, as a result, more than six years have gone by while they are still working to complete their cultural change. While change may be implemented fairly quickly, it takes consistent leadership commitment at all levels to complete the institutionalization process.

Organizational change can be seen as a double-edged management sword. Any major economic, social or professional event in an organization can disrupt the flow of business and other functions within the organization. When change occurs, it can promote unity and tighter integration throughout the organization, or unleash a backlash of unrest and turbulence. Changes in a large enough organization can affect an entire industry. For instance, when we look at the sharp decline in crude oil prices in late 1998, we see that such event caused a significant reduction of business opportunities for oil service companies. By the same token, the burst of the dotcom bubble also brought hard changes to marketing companies and the whole concept of real estate on the Internet. The knowledge economy is being characterized by as capitalizing on change, and unless organizations get ready for it, the price to be paid can be very high, as this new economic condition calls for boldness, innovation, and risk-taking.

One of my favorite places in the world to spend time is in Brazil. After I spend time there with family and friends, I am always amazed with the Brazilian economy and how it positions itself within the global market. What I admire is the wiliness and ability of Brazilian entrepreneurs to adapt to change. With the economy in a challenging and ever-evolving position, how do Brazilian leaders pull this off over and over again? The answer, very likely, is heavily focused on innovation, as executives respond to the challenge by trying to improve their marketing focus and *selling their way* out of the downturn. They see the move of their *cheese* -- by global market forces, inflation, and hyperactive cultural changes -- as an opportunity to innovate, re-inventing themselves. The same goes for Mexico, one of the leaders in the use of smartcard technology in the world. I am definitely convinced that Brazilian entrepreneurs are always aware that they

---

[4] In Knowledge Enabled Enterprise Architecture white paper at http://strategy-partners.com

must change or adapt to new market forces, when the market environment changes, in order to continuously bring business success. That is why I believe it is the scariest markets that prove the mettle of a fund and its managers.

CKOs should use their deeper knowledge about KM, community of practices and organizational change to help in teaching organizations to navigate the *maze* of change, and to reorganize their organizational groups, much like an NFL coach reorganizes his team over and over again, as many times as necessary, according to the game at hand. Thus the organizational positions, reporting lines and responsibilities of all executive staff, senior managers, and departmental groups must be modified according to the challenge, to better address the situation. Under Spencer's analogy, that is when the organization must *move the cheese*.

Changing One Step at a Time

Changes in an organization not only take time, but also many steps. In the process, any attempt to shorten the steps or develop short cuts will only produce a false illusion of speed, and the results are never satisfactory. Change is at the core of the gap between know-how and how-to in any organization, and I believe the gap often exists because leaders know how to implement a change, but don't feel easy about how to implement it, as they avoid dealing with changes. Thus CKOs must help executives and leaders to realize that change is not only necessary to bridge the gap, but also the only constant they can count on when turning knowledge into action.

Whether it is bridging the gap between the know-how of a new technology and the how-to incorporate such technology, about the know-how of achieving compliance with a new regulation and how-to implement it, change is the bridge that makes it possible. Know-how must generate strategies, but only change strategies will provide the execution plans of how-to create effective and lasting organizational change to meet these challenges, as depicted in figure 2.3.

Figure 2.3 – Change is the bridge, the constant connecting know-how and how-to in the transformation of knowledge into action

Changes can come in many forms and forces originated from both inside and outside the organization. Bridging a knowledge gap within an organization will always require the implementation of new organizational structures, realignment and often consolidation of organizational roles and responsibilities, and even the revision and restatement of the company's mission. Thus change is always at the core of bridging knowledge gaps, of turning knowledge into action. The problem is, leaders and senior executives often have the tendency to postpone change, typically through such strategies as "crossing that bridge when it comes," which often turns into not crossing the bridge at all, or worse, burning the bridge! That's why expensive consulting recommendations seldom lead to change, as executives, despite knowing what needs to be done – often even before hiring a consultant! — are not ready to embrace the changes that will come about as they begin crossing the bridge of know-how into how-to.

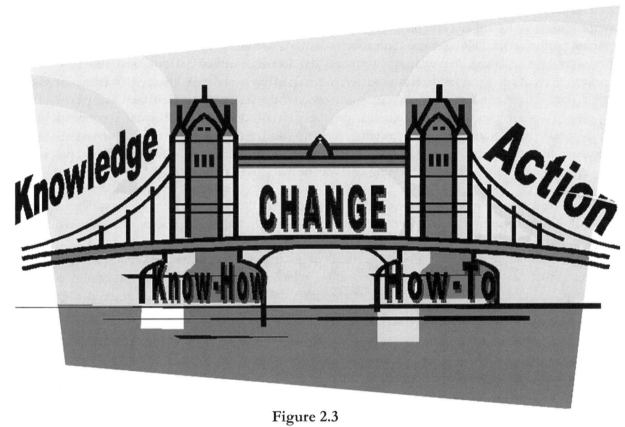

Figure 2.3

Changes are easier and more likely at the early phases of the project life cycle than at the completion. Stakeholders can have a greater influence on the outcome of the project deliverables in the early phases, but in the final phases of the project life cycle, their influence on change diminishes. Thankfully, as depicted in Figure 2.4, changes at the beginning of the project generally cost less and have lower risk than changes at the end of a project.

Figure 2.4 – Dealing with change

As John Kotter[5] states, one of the major mistakes corporations commit is not to establish a great enough sense of urgency in changing. "Most successful change efforts begin when some individuals or some groups start to look hard at a company's competitive situation, market position, technological trends and financial performance," Kotter says. Surprisingly enough, according to Kotter, more than 50% of the companies he saw failing in the changing process did so because they did not have enough sense of urgency. Executives either underestimated the hardships that come with changes, in particular taking people out of their comfort zone, or they overestimated the sense of urgency they had placed in the process. Lack of patience, immobilization in the face of downside possibilities, concerns about defensiveness from senior employees, lowering of morale, and outlooks of short-term business results are all reasons for not embracing change, not wanting to cross the bridge, or as Spencer would put it, not wanting to deal with the fact that something or someone has moved the cheese.

CKOs are leaders, and leaders lead, or co-lead, in particular in times of change. To do so, they must be aware of the intricacies and inner workings of the groups they interact with, or lead. Although leading can be exciting and challenging, in times of major changes it can be very frustrating; organizations are made up of people, and human behavior can be very difficult, if not impossible, to predict. Change always requires the creation of new systems; it requires innovation, which is a great thing. But innovation demands leadership. Therefore, before CKOs can readily help the implementation of change in a group or organization, they must first understand what makes an organization tick.

Needless to say, if of the right breed, CKOs can very well be the best professionals for the job, better suited than CIOs and CTOs, as (hopefully) they are aware of the organizational culture, including artifacts, values, and assumptions, and framed to gain an insight and understanding of the organization. Of course, CKOs can also be great co-leaders, but they rely on the support of their leader, namely the CEO. Change will only really happen when the organization has a good leader, often a new leader, who genuinely sees the need for major changes.

---

[5] In Leading Change: Why Transformation Efforts Fail, Harvard Business Review on Change, 1998, Boston

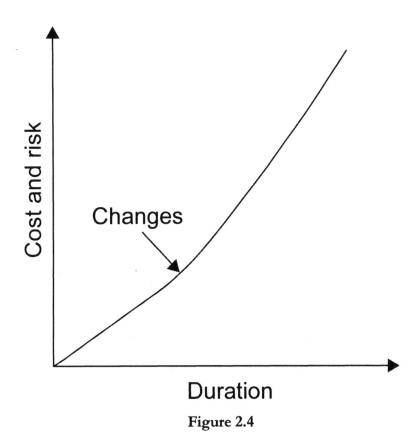

Figure 2.4

Most Common Mistakes Made by Executive Sponsors

According to data from the 2005 Change Management Best Practice Report,[6] active and visible executive sponsorship is the number one contributor to change management success. The top three mistakes made by executive sponsors, as cited by the report participants, were:

1. Executive sponsors failed to personally engage as the sponsor for the change:

   - They abdicated sponsorship to lower level managers, the project team or consultants.

   - They failed to communicate the need for change and risks of not changing.

   - They were absent or ignored the project, failed to stay involved and track progress, and were not visible after the initial kick off.

   - They failed to reinforce a consistent message throughout the project.

2. Executive sponsors changed priorities mid-stream:

   - Their commitment wavered or support dwindled.

   - Other projects took priority.

   - They moved on to the next "flavor of the month."

3. Executive sponsors did not build a sponsorship coalition:

   - They assumed support from other business leaders would be there; they moved too fast without ensuring that key managers were on board.

   - They underestimated resistance and the impact of the change on employees.

   - They assumed the message trickled down; they assumed everyone understood the need for change.

   - They failed to set expectations of other business leaders.

   - They tolerated resistance from mid-level managers.

Participants also listed other mistakes that executive sponsors made during major change initiatives.

   - They did not recognize the need for change management early in the project.

---

[6] Excerpted from the 2005 Change Management Best Practice Report, available at www.prosci.com.

- They dictated the change with little or no communication.

- They did not see change leadership as a skill gap among managers and business leaders.

- They failed to identify and manage change overload (too many changes all at one time causing employees to reach change saturation).

- They rushed the change without adequate preparation and planning.

- They let the project move along without celebrating milestones; they failed to acknowledge efforts and express appreciation for efforts upon completion of the project.

Chapter 3
Overcoming Emotional Obstacles

Success often involves a strong internal champion, stumping for change.

What are the barriers you are likely to face in attempting to build (or rebuild!) your team and implement a change management plan? These barriers are real, and they exist in every team. A typical example is the structural barriers of hierarchical teams, such as departments, groups and divisions, etc. Operating companies in different countries, languages and cultures often presents barriers as well. There are many more barriers in building a team that will tend to be multicultural and geographically displaced, and you must take the time to identify them, and have a strategy to overcome them, prior to any knowledge transferring initiative.

In order for any change management initiative to be successful, you must not focus your efforts on a specific team, but on the whole organization, across all of those interdepartmental barriers. To do this you will have to focus on increasing the ability of team members to communicate their thoughts to others in the team, as the collective result of a lot of individual actions would be necessary to produce a single result for the entire corporation. As depicted in Figure 3.1, you must make sure to communicate the vision of the changing plan clearly, emphasizing the strategic sense in a way that you inspire others, with passion. If you come across as not believing in the plan, why would they? The question is how do you increase the power of these individuals in sharing their thoughts with others in the team?

Figure 3.1 – Requirements for an effective change management process

There are many areas you should concentrate on in attempting to develop your change management team, and striving to transfer knowledge at the same time. Two of the main areas of attack should be:

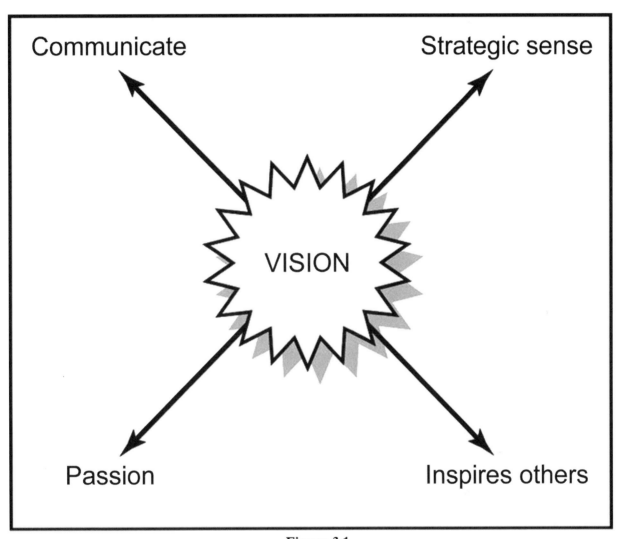

Communicate

Strategic sense

VISION

Passion

Inspires others

Figure 3.1

- Increasing the power of individuals in sharing their thoughts

- Overcoming the team's organization barriers

Increasing the Power of Individuals in Sharing Their Thoughts

Typically, most teams gather information on the front line, and then pass it to someone next to them up the line. The process then continues further up the line, with each individual team member adding some perspective to make it better. Finally it reaches some guru, typically an executive, an officer within the organization, who gives the information the benefit of his infinite wisdom. Then the information starts coming back down the line or is stored into the knowledge base, the memory, of the company. Curious enough, in many cases the originator of the information will not recognize the information when it gets back to him and, worse still, the information will not communicate what he had intended. If there was a system in place that could let the individual with the need for knowledge talk directly with the individual or group that has the latest and best knowledge, then this whole confusion could be eliminated.

For a change management plan to be effective, it is essential for team members to be able to clearly communicate what they need, so that the individual providing the information will be able to provide a rapid response to them. Your organization needs to understand, as depicted in Figure 3.3, that change begins with breakthrough thinking. You can accomplish this by radically changing the span of communication of the individual, from within his immediate work group to the entire team and beyond, to anybody on any network that they go to for information. The greatest database in the team is housed in its members' minds, and that is where the power of the team actually resides. These individual knowledge bases are continually changing and adapting to the real world in front of them.

Figure 3.2 – Change begins with breakthrough thinking

Major change initiatives can fail. The main reasons for these failures are:

- A fuzzy, poorly defined definition of the future state

- Failure to integrate all major initiatives into a master plan

- Lack of a structured approach to address the human issues surrounding the deployment of a new initiative

- Lack of top management support for the initiative

It is the role of the team leader to make sure to connect these individual knowledge bases together, bridging the knowledge gap and avoiding those failure-causing situations above, so that the team can do whatever they do best in the shortest possible time, and without the risk of knowledge loss. I strongly believe that the greater the span of communication and collaboration that you give to team members, the

BREAKTHROUGH THINKING

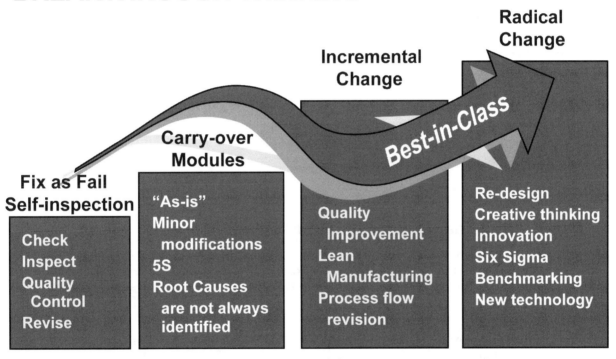

Radical
Change

Incremental
Change

Best-in-Class

**Fix as Fail
Self-inspection**

Check
Inspect
Quality
Control
Revise

**Carry-over
Modules**

"As-is"
Minor
modifications
5S
Root Causes
are not always
identified

Quality
Improvement
Lean
Manufacturing
Process flow
revision

Re-design
Creative thinking
Innovation
Six Sigma
Benchmarking
New technology

Figure 3.2

greater the span of influence in the changing process they will have. The greater the span of influence, the more powerful the individual will be. If the span of communication is limited to a small horizon, such as a work group on a local network, then the influence that the individuals can bring to bear will be minimal, the change will be minimal, and the benefits to the organization will also be minimal.

As you expand the ability of the individual members of the team, you expand the ability of the organization to change. As you change the span of influence of the team member, you change the power of the member and of the team as well. Buckman Laboratories, for example, were very successful in this strategy. They increased the span of communication of their individual associates from their immediate teams to the global world of the company and any place else they needed to go for information. They gave their people access to the world, both inside and outside of the company.

It is this change in the span of communication of team members that provides the basis of the cultural change that organizations are experiencing worldwide. At Buckman, all those individuals that have something intelligent to say now have a forum in which to say it. Management can no longer hold them back. These people became noticed and respected in the organization based on what they were able to contribute to others, not how well they could please some boss. Furthermore, those that will not or cannot contribute also become noticeable, and can be intelligently eliminated from the team and the organization.

Therefore, if you want your team to be more open to the changing process and increase its power in the marketplace, increase the span of communication, collaboration and knowledge transfer of the members of the team. Allow them to talk to whomever they need to for information. This is how you can improve the speed of response to the customer.

Overcoming Team's Emotional Barriers

Team's emotional barriers are the major factor responsible for the knowledge gap within teams. The collection of minds that exists within teams across corporate barriers, geographic barriers, cultural, and language barriers are great. It is necessarily to effectively transfer knowledge across time and space to meet the needs of the learning organization and, ultimately, their customers.

Ideally, the knowledge transfer between the teams and its customers, as well as among themselves, should happen instantly. But this is not an easy task, one near to impossible to fulfill, unless in very specific environments. But if you can reduce the transferring time, the feedback, from weeks and days to a few hours, or no more than a day, than you have achieved a major milestone in knowledge transferring. The speed of response is a very important and measurable aspect of a successful knowledge transfer, in particular at the furthermost reaches of the corporation. This is because fast response time can drastically eliminate distance.

When you quickly provide feedback to another member of your team or a customer in a timely fashion, the distance between you, your office or your company and the customer becomes irrelevant. That's why many help desk systems and customer support services outsourced overseas, mainly in India, are being so successful. (Many aren't as well, but for other reasons, such as inability to absorb local neologisms and cultural nuances.). The customer in United States doesn't really care if the solution to the problem is coming from the next town over or from overseas. All the customer cares about is that the necessary knowledge is transferred in a timely fashion.

Fostering a Culture of Change

Boards of directors and executive staff are responsible for the climate they create in the organization; the same is true for team leaders and their teams. Such climate has a major impact on the team's ability to change across time and space. Over the years I have seen this as the most difficult aspect of the change management process in any organization. By default, people have always taught themselves to collect knowledge over the years as a way to achieve power, or as a way of professional self-preservation, to say the least. What is taught in colleges and universities is that knowledge should be acquired and used, but we are never taught how to share it. If teams are to be successful in a change management process, we must reverse this tendency by leading the change process effectively, as depicted in Figure 3.4.

Figure 3.3 – Seven Steps for Leading Change

Sustainable organizational change happens when the following dimensions are aligned and developed in balance:

- Business

    o Making sense of the strategic context

    o Defining a compelling picture of the future which engages people's hearts and minds

    o Shaping and deploying strategies and objectives to make the vision become a reality

- Process

    o Optimizing the business processes which develop and deliver services and products

    o Ensuring that the management processes which provide direction, support and challenge for staff are robust and aligned

- Social

    o Creating a culture in which individuals and teams want to, can and do deliver excellent results

    o Ensuring people have the skills to be successful

    o Ensuring the organizational structure supports people doing what needs to be done.

33

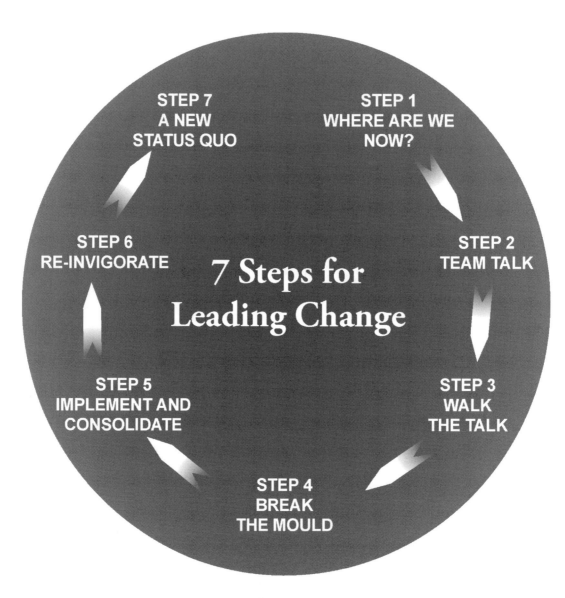

Figure 3.3

In this new economy, the most powerful individuals will not be those building their own "info-islands," but those that are willing to change when necessary, and to help their peers and teams as a whole in the process by proactively sharing what they know. Continuity and trust, so necessary to accomplish proactive knowledge transferring within teams, must be promoted. Further, this same climate of continuity and trust should also be fostered with customers.

Another important aspect to consider is with regard to the quality of the professionals that you, as a team leader, can bring to relationships with partners, supply chains and distribution channels. This will determine the level at which your entire organization can operate in these relationships. The higher the quality of the individuals engaged in this knowledge transfer and changing process, the higher the quality of the knowledge that can be brought to bear on any problem that your customers and co-workers bring to you. But don't underestimate other levels of the organization, as every professional, independent of their role, can effectively contribute to this change management and knowledge transfer initiative. At Buckman laboratories, their goal was to have 80 percent of the organization effectively engaged on the front line.

Such change in the level of knowledge sharing/transferring assumes different shapes depending on the organization where it is implemented. It may translate, as in Buckman's case, as how to get as many team members as possible creating and transferring as much knowledge as possible, in the best way possible, in order to have a positive impact on the customer. Some teams may focus on making sure that there is a high level of interaction between the organization's members and paying customers for a measurable frequency and duration. For others, it might be to ensure that the majority of their team members actively use their electronic forums, web portals, chats, instant messaging and email, or even to ensure that they get their accounting right, which may include profit recovery activities, so that their groups measure up to this new corporate goal.

My advice is, no matter what the nuances, idiosyncrasies and specifics of an organization, the goal of change management strategies is to bring about the full weight of the knowledge that exists in the hardware, software and team members, in a relevant and useful manner, to bear upon the requirements of the customer and the marketplace. I believe that any team, as change agents, especially those that realized they must adopt a generative learning attitude versus an adaptive one, are doing a lot of these things already. But if they can get all of their people exercising knowledge transfer at all times, a tremendous power can be unleashed. The goal here is not to go after definitions, numbers, procedures or any other quantifiable business goals. It should be to promote team member involvement, commitment, creativity, passion, and ultimately the freedom to do everything the team can, and to use all of the knowledge it has, to make sure that they have done their best to satisfy their customers--inside and outside the organization--in all areas.

To bring order to chaos, and reduce the emotional barriers raised by professionals inside the organization, organize the change process effort into three coordinated campaigns:

- Political Campaign - Without a political campaign, an initiative risks being undermined. So,

  o Forge Alliances

  o Pass the Baton

- Shift Structures

- Marketing Campaign - Without a marketing campaign, a leader will be dismissed as a social engineer out of touch with employees. So,

  - Listen In

  - Work with Lead Customers

  - Develop a Theme

- Military Campaign – Fifty percent of all corporate initiatives bog down simply because people stop paying attention to them. So,

  - Secure Supply Lines

  - Choose Beachheads

  - Create a War Room

Most successful executives launch these three campaigns simultaneously rather than sequentially. Knowledge transferring through a change management process will only be successful when you are able to fully and effectively engage all of your team members, with a change system and within cultural surroundings where they can all be comfortable practicing it, with emotional barriers lowered. Only then you will have sufficiently addressed the collaboration and knowledge transferring issues of your team.

Promoting Innovation by Thinking Out of the Box

By nature team leaders are, and should be, professionals capable of influencing others. The multi-disciplinary background team leaders must have greatly enhances their span of influence, during times of change, over diverse teams inside the organization and out. Therefore, team leaders today must be instrumental in bridging knowledge gaps inside their teams, in order to achieve faster growth of the talented people in the company, to promote new ideas and innovative thinking, and ultimately to help the learning organization to think out of the box. Such professionals can influence others across time and space with a resulting increase in morale as well.

Team leaders are not the only ones responsible for fostering innovation among the team. Many other professionals within the organization also contribute, beginning with the Board, executive staff and technologists. The fact is, everyone in a learning organization should be able to promote innovation within the teams. The important thing to realize is that, to achieve these benefits, everyone in the team must accept the fact that radical and rapid change will be part of the learning organization's life. Thus, consider these best practices facts:

- No matter who or where team members are in the world, everyone should be able to contribute to change management solutions in the organization, regardless of its nature or where it occurs. The challenge is to structure the team to recognize this fact. Another challenge is to structure this new learning team around the flow of knowledge, rather than geography.

- You must be sure to build teams that trust each other so that they can function effectively without an office, a department, a central core. This means to enable team members to be effective even while roaming; at a hotel room, at home, at the airport, at a satellite office. In other words, you must be able to move the team (and the office!) to where the people experiencing change are, anywhere and anytime. Done? Now it is time to move the entire organization to wherever it is needed at any point in time-- without affecting the knowledge flow.

- In this new knowledge economy, where customers are much more aware of sales and service processes, speed in responding to them is vital if you want to remain competitive in the marketplace. Thus, here you have another challenge: to make sure the farthest groups and individuals within your team have the same speed of response as everyone else.

- Every individual's ability to acquire and use knowledge is very important to any change management process. Therefore, the quality of the professionals you hire is critical to the future of this new learning team. The cumulative knowledge of the individual team members determines how well the team will function. In this process, watch for reactions coming from the human resources group. You may find your organization needs to hire teachers and coaches.

- If everybody is critically important to the organization's ability to close the gap between the know-how of the organization and the how-to serve the customer, then what needs to happen so that the minds of your associates can be expanded, so that they can be the best that they can be? Ask yourself how you can deliver learning anytime, anywhere. You may rely on programs such as The Learning Space, developed by The Lotus Institute as an application under Lotus Notes and the Global Campus initiative of IBM, or even this author's site, MGCGOnline, by MGCG, at www.mgcgonline.com. Organizations like these offer a variety of courses, and they may also customize one for you, at no extra charge.

To reap the benefits of change management, you should invest in it like any other investment that will change the organization. It requires active entrepreneurial support, from the Board and executive staff down to junior associates. Knowledge transfer, as well as knowledge management as a whole, resumes in culture change. If you want culture change in a team, then the head of that team has to lead it. This means the team leader needs to hold the flag by adopting the changes, by using the latest hardware and software for communications, by being open and accepting changes.

Remember, everybody in the team (and the organization as a whole) will be watching. If the team leader does not walk the walk, then the rest of the team will not see it as important and will not adopt the changes either. Make sure that whatever statement of direction you have, it is backed up with actions; otherwise, nothing will happen in the organization.

Therefore, keep in mind that change management is more than collaboration with industry on specific products or technologies with commercial potential. It is a long-term process that establishes symbiotic ties between industrial and academic researchers. Transfer of knowledge during this process can be achieved through education, outreach, publications, workshops, and an array of other means.

Having a Code of Ethics

A code of ethics is the glue that holds a change management team, any organization for that matter, together. It provides the basis for the respect and trust that are necessary in a change management process. These fundamental beliefs are crucial for communication and collaboration across the many barriers to change management that exist in any organization. A sound (and realistic) code of ethics should be seen as an integral part of the effort to achieve and maintain the change management process in a learning organization.

Taking Buckman Laboratories again as an example, a clear code of ethics was key in their change management implementation, because they were separated by many miles, and diversity of cultures and languages. This required a clear understanding of the basic principles by which they would operate. Some of these basic principles may include, but should not be limited to:

- A forward looking attitude about the future of the team should be constantly nurtured, so that generative learning, instead of adaptive, can take place, allowing team members inside the team to proactively control their destiny instead of letting events overtake them.

- All decisions should be made according to what is right for the good of the whole team rather than what is expedient in a given situation.

- Customers, and their total satisfaction, should be the only reason for the existence of any learning organization, and any team that embodies it. To serve them properly, the team must supply products and services which provide economic benefit over and above their cost.

- Each member's contributions and accomplishments should be recognized and rewarded.

- Learning teams are made up of individual members, each of whom has different capabilities and potentials, all of which are necessary to the success of the company.

- Individuality should be acknowledged by treating each other with dignity and respect, striving to maintain continuous and positive communications among everyone within the team.

- The highest ethics must be used to guide the team's business dealings, to ensure that every member within the team is always proud to be a part of the team.

- The only way to provide high quality products and services to customers is to be driven by a total customer satisfaction motto -- not by fear of being let go, or by personal gains -- in everything the team does.

- The team's standards should always be upheld by the individuals and by the corporation as a whole, so that everyone may be respected as professional contributors and as a team.

- The responsibilities of corporate and individual citizenship should always be discharged in order to earn and maintain the respect of the teams.

- There should be a policy of providing work for all members, no matter what the prevailing business conditions may be.

Chapter 4
Planning Change

Executive sponsors often fail to personally engage as the sponsor for change.

There is no debate on the matter that change is a necessity. But the implementation of the change process will always limit the effectiveness and motivation needed to lead. There are six key elements that must be addressed that are essential to creating the business/educational change that an organization needs to implement change.

Figure 4.1 depicts what typically happens with most change management plans. At first, the morale level of the organization tends to be fairly good (notice that is not high, due to onset resistance), and during the first stages of the change implementation, it even increases. That increase in morale is not due to successful results, as we already understand that change management results tend to be slow, to take time. The reason for the increase is denial of the difficulties that lie ahead, combined with false expectations. One it is realized that expectations previous are unattainable, there is a sharp drop into the "pit of despair." As the change process continues people resist, but ultimately a "grudging acceptance" occurs. Eventually there will be a feeling of relief, and business as usual sets in.

Figure 4.1 – Leading Change: Why Transformation Efforts Fail

Therefore, not only it is very import to have effective planning for change, but also to try to anticipate the possible results of failing, in order to direct time and effort to each element. The diagram in Figure 4.2 is a useful diagnostic tool to help identify an area of focus in a business, classroom, school, district or agency. It may also be used as a planning tool which highlights areas that should be addressed prior to the implementation of any new program or system change. Leadership must be present throughout the entire process. From whatever point you find yourself at, leaders must assume responsibility for removing barriers to correcting the problems.

Figure 4.2 – Assessing and Planning Change

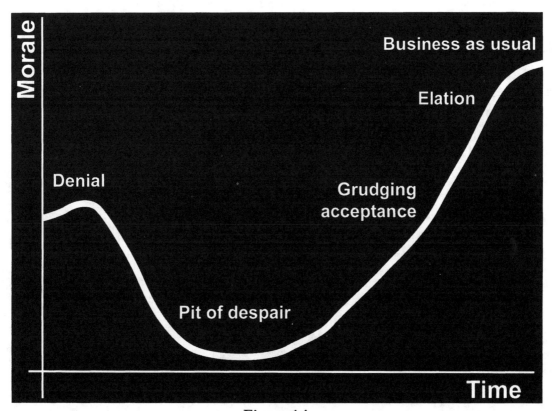

Figure 4.1

41

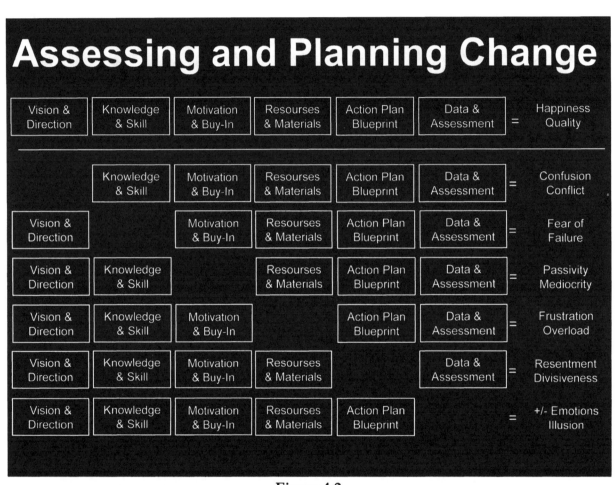

Figure 4.2

Effective planning for change includes six major components that will reduce fear and allow workers more opportunities to find satisfaction in their new changed processes, which translates to better relationships and a more productive workforce.

Vision and Direction

"Aim," "purpose," and "values" are all terms that are used for vision and direction. They relate directly to the notion that everyone must be focused on the Constancy of Purpose (Deming). This is primarily the leader's responsibility. Without a common purpose, people will do their job to the best of their ability "as they understand it." Therein lies the problem; if everyone is working hard, but working in opposite or contradictory directions, there will be little cohesion for the group. The group, whether an individual class or a school district, will be unfocused and confused as to what is expected.

In addition, the group should be ready to accept responsibility for their actions. In my experience, this has to cover a multitude of areas, including:

- Identifying and targeting individuals in the team

- Knowing the barriers in the team-building effort

- Having a code of ethics

- Fostering culture change

- Promoting innovation by thinking out of the box

Identifying and Targeting Individuals in the Team

For any successful change planning process, it is important for you to identify the individuals (not only processes) you need to change. Unfortunately, I find that the more important the change process is, the more difficult it is to identify and locate these professionals in the team, never mind getting them to believe and support the changing process. Take for instance global consulting companies; locating their professionals can be hard at times. If you were to weigh the average amount of time professional consultants spend between offices across the country and around the world at any point in time, you would find that 86 percent of them are outside the office, and many times outside the country.

In a team where the office is not the place where business is conducted, change management can be a very hard job to accomplish. The same is true for any other team, although maybe not at such high levels as the professional consulting industry. For instance, if I am in my office for 40 hours a week, then my time in the office represents less than 25 percent of my total available time that week. If I consider the times I am working from home or a hotel room, then the percentage of time in the office falls even further. Among the big four consulting firms, you will find that their consultants are in the office less than 14 percent of their available time.

Therefore, knowing where your team members are and how they will contribute to the change management process is very important, and must be taken into consideration before you establish a change management team and strategy.

Alignment

Alignment is crucial! As Bill O'Brien, Former CEO of Hanover Insurance Company stated, "To empower people in an unaligned organization can be counter-productive. Unless people share the same 'mental models' about the business reality in which they operate, empowering people increases the burden of management to maintain coherence and direction."[1]

Values, like the Aim, Purpose and Vision, must be embedded into the organization. In successful companies and market leaders, the day-to-day management focus on the delivery of customer values is tantamount to organizational success. The organizational values must become guiding principles for major decisions and the day-to-day operations. As Yogi Berra, Hall of Fame member and former catcher for the New York Yankees once said, "If you don't know where you're going, you might end up someplace else." How true this is for organizations in the change process that lose their aim or fragment their efforts?

Knowledge and Skills

Providing everyone with the necessary knowledge and skills for the change process is, obviously, a necessity. In practice, however, this is not understood and/or properly resourced. Initial training is seldom the problem. A lack of understanding of the time, complexity of the knowledge and skills, and appropriate follow-up creates an inequality of knowledge and an excessive variation in skill and ability. An additional pitfall is assuming that the workers have the requisite knowledge and skills to engage in the change process, just because they were employed and have the right credentials. Everyone must receive the training that they need to perform the job that is expected of them.

Workers need to comprehend all of these components to be properly trained and highly effective. How else will they be able to be productive in helping to improve the system, unless they understand the function of all departments, not just their own?

Additional skills which must be emphasized include problem-solving, conflict-resolution and relationship-building. If people don't know how to get along, cooperate and work for the good of the system, there will not be much chance of becoming a market leader.

---

[1] A Conversation With Bill O'Brien, excerpted from an interview with Roger Breisch, July 1998, Entre Nous, a publication of MOLN (http://www.williamjobrien.org/Docs_PDFs/Entre%20Nous.pdf)

Motivation and Buy-In

Motivation and buy-in refers to the belief that the change will improve teaching and learning. The aim and purpose are closely tied to the motivation and buy-in. The program implementation and/or changes must be consistent with the aim of the system. Leaders that are congruent in action and words increase the belief that this specific change process will be embraced.

Customers and employees want to know "How does what you want me to do benefit me?" The answer to this question, in most cases, will have a direct correlation to the amount of "Motivation and Buy-In" to all of the components identified in this chapter. Throughout the change process, everyone should see opportunities for a greater sense of belonging, accomplishment and recognition, freedom of expression, creativity and enjoyment. These needs must be addressed in order to provide the motivation to continue through difficult, sometimes tedious, times. Additionally, people want to know that their hard work and dedication will be not only recognized, but remembered.

Resources

Resources refer to the commitment and delivery of time, money and materials to create and implement the change. This is often planned for initially, but as budget cuts and new priorities occur, it is imperative that management creates contingency plans to help "stay the course" and provide long-term resources. Although this may be the simplest of the components to present and understand, it is not always easy to find or provide all of the necessary resources.

Action Plans

A well-written plan is essential for long-term change. Leaders often assume that everyone understands the "how" and "why" of continual improvement plans. As with vision and direction, it is the leader's responsibility to continually emphasize, focus on and/or remind others of the plans that are in place. The plan should include, but not be restricted to, the following questions:

- How will we implement and/or change?

- How is this program or change consistent with our aim or purpose?

- What will be implemented or changed?

- How will the implementation take place? What are the steps?

- What knowledge and/or skills do we need?

- What do we already have?

- What will we need to acquire?

- What is the motivation or buy-in?

- What resources will be needed?

- How much time is needed?

- By when? What is the deadline?

- How much money is needed?

- What materials, technology, etc. are needed?

Feedback, Assessment & Data

This would appear to be an obvious component, but meaningful data is not always a priority, nor is it always easy to come by. Without data to tell us how we are doing, we have an illusion of effectiveness. One need only look at the technology field to know that what was once effective is now obsolete. The idea of building a quality product and counting on it to provide long-term revenue in today's technologically advanced market is laughable. Not only does the product become technologically obsolete, the price drops dramatically when newer products are released.

The following questions are provided as a guideline for determining what data is needed and how to collect it:

- Are we doing what we say we are doing? How do we know?

- Is what we are doing cost-effective?

- Who has the information that we need?

- What is the best method (statistics, surveys, etc.) of gathering the data?

- What data do we have to support the need for change?

- What data do we have to support the projected effectiveness of this change?

- What data do we need to collect to determine the effectiveness for our program?

The purpose of data is not to place blame, but to determine if the organization is on course to accomplish its goals in a manner that is consistent with the Aim, Purpose and Values.

Some organizations may find themselves lacking in several of these areas. This is not uncommon. The list above was intended to help determine where a group or department is in the change process. Dr. Deming taught that up to 95% of all our problems are based in system difficulties. With that in mind, the list is not intended to find fault with others, only to identify any components that must be addressed to continually improve teaching and learning. It is the responsibility of all concerned to work together to correct any deficiencies or "holes" in their processes. As Henry Ford was quoted on many occasions, "Don't find fault, find remedy."[2]

Planning a Starting and Focal Point for Change

In planning for change, processes and realistic time frames must be considered. With that in mind, the discussion and evaluation of the three E's can be helpful in creating both a starting point and a focal point for change.

The Three E's

Environment refers to the physically and psychologically safe environment that is necessary for quality work and self-evaluation to occur. We are talking about focusing on creating an environment where professionals in phase of change are comfortable and willing to take the risks necessary to learn and grow. A common practice that does not help to eliminate the fear of failure, or create a trusting environment, is to ask workers to try to solve a problem with which they are struggling. When they comply and their attempt to resolve the problem is unsuccessful, they are still not achieving successful results.

Expectations of the quality of the changing process must be managed, discussed and displayed. Workers must learn what quality work is, as well as how to demonstrate and explain how the knowledge and skills are useful to them.

Evaluation refers to the team members developing the skill of assessing their work. In conjunction with the proper environment and expectations, this can be accomplished through self-evaluation or concurrent evaluation (with the team leader).

In assisting others through the change process, it is helpful to put these three areas on a continuum, as depicted in Figure 4.3. This enables people to look at where they are in the process and to determine if they are moving in the right direction.

Figure 4.3 – Planning a starting and focal point for change

Because change is difficult, the questions that one must ask for continuous improvement are:

1. Are we taking advantage of opportunities to include others in creating a positive, supportive environment?

---

[2] Ford, H. (1988). Today and Tomorrow, Productivity Press, New York, p32.

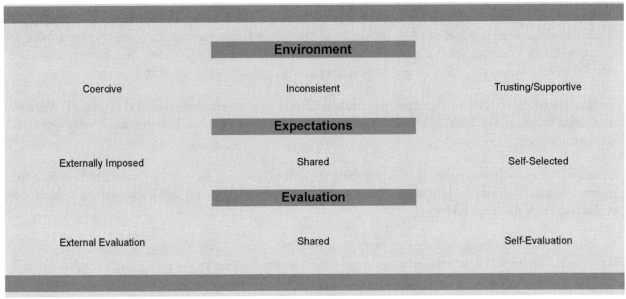

Figure 4.3

2. What are we doing to create an environment that is positive, supportive and encourages risk-taking?

3. Are we taking advantage of opportunities to include others in setting expectations and discussing quality?

4. What are we doing to teach our professionals to create quality work?

5. Are we taking advantage of opportunities to include others in concurrent-evaluation?

6. Are we taking advantage of opportunities to ask others to evaluate their work?

7. What are we doing to evaluate the environment, expectations and evaluation of our classrooms, school and/or district?

In discussing and evaluating the Three E's, there are many questions that can be asked to help change agents evaluate where they are, and where they would like to be, in the above continuum. In order to move toward quality learning, all segments of the learner population must be invited to participate, given the freedom to feel invested, and provided the support to excel. There are three key evaluative questions that every organization must address:

- Is our change process plan beneficial for the organization?

- Are we offering every professional an opportunity for quality learning?

- Are we working hard to ensure that every learner grasps the opportunity?

An organization's products and services are a result of the quality of its professionals' learning and skill sets; whether the consumer of that product is a college, an employer, or society at large, a well-educated, motivated student is desired.

Deming's Chain Reaction in Business[3] offers a good model for basing change planning. Improvement in the quality of an organization eliminates much of the waste of human and material resources. There are fewer defects and therefore the system operates more efficiently and effectively, due to less reworking. Change management plan should address:

1. Improvement of Quality

2. Costs Decreases

---

[3]Deming. E. (2000). Out of the Crisis, The MIT Press, Boston, p63.

3. Productivity Increases

    - Less rework

    - Fewer failures

    - Discipline problems decrease

    - Better use of time

4. Cost-Effective System

    - Expanded opportunities

    - Professionals stay engaged in learning

5. Organization promotes and retains responsible, productive professionals

There are many reasons to follow Deming's second management point of "Adopt the New Philosophy." The engagement of everyone in the organization in the quest toward quality of service is imperative. Masaki Imai, in his book Kaizen, declares "Let there be no mistake: quality is management's responsibility, and poor quality is the result of poor management."[4]

---

[4] Kaizen (1986). The Key to Japan's Competitive Success, McGraw-Hill, New York, p. 121.

Chapter 5
Managing Change

Employees are better able to tolerate change if they understand why the change is important, and if they feel the changes are being handled with fairness and transparency.

There are eight basic lessons that can be learned about the process of managing change:

- You can't mandate what matters - The more complex the change, the less you can force it

- Change is a journey, not a blueprint - Change is non-linear, loaded with uncertainty and excitement, and sometimes perverse

- Problems are our friends - Problems are inevitable and you can't learn without them

- Vision and strategic planning come later - Premature visions and planning blind and bias change

- Individualism and collectivism must have equal power - There are no one-sided solutions; neither isolation nor group thinking should dominate

- Neither centralization nor decentralization works - Both top-down and bottom-up strategies are necessary

- Connection with the wider environment is critical for success - The best organizations learn externally as well as internally

- Every person is a change agent - Change is too important to leave to the experts; each individual's personal mind set and mastery are the ultimate tools for change.

As you analyze these eight lessons, realize that there is a pattern underlying these dynamic change factors, and it concerns people's ability to work with polar opposites:

- Simultaneously pushing for change while allowing self-learning to unfold

- Being prepared for a journey of uncertainty

- Seeing problems as sources of creative resolution

- Having a vision, but not being blinded by it

- Valuing the individual and the group

- Incorporating centralizing and decentralizing forces

- Being internally cohesive, but externally oriented

- Valuing personal change agentry as the route to system change

In essence, change takes place on three levels, as depicted in figure 5.1: The self, the team or the small organization, and the wider system that surrounds the team, the small organization or the organizational unit - depending how you define the system borders. In a process, learning needs to be facilitated on all three levels to become sustainable.

Figure 5.1 - Levels of Change

Managing change is very important, as change will only happen if the following dimensions are aligned and developed in balance, as shown in Figure 5.2:

- Business

  o Making sense of the strategic context

  o Defining a compelling picture of the future which engages people's hearts and minds

  o Shaping and deploying strategies and objectives to make the vision become a reality

- Process

  o Optimizing the business processes which develop and deliver services and products

  o Ensuring that the management processes which provide direction, support and challenge for staff are robust and aligned

- Social

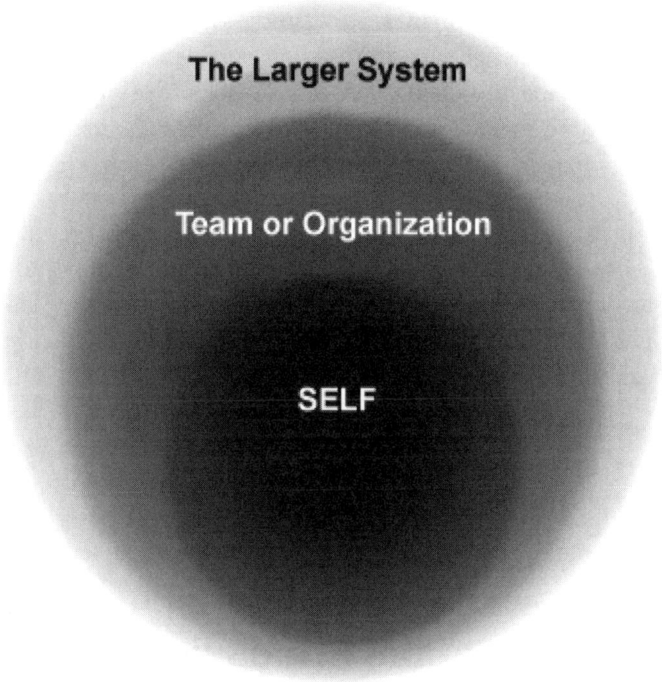

The Larger System

Team or Organization

SELF

Figure 5.1

o   Creating a culture in which individuals and teams want to, can and do deliver excellent results

o   Ensuring people have the <u>skills to be successful</u>

o   Ensuring the organizational structure supports people doing what needs to be done.

Figure 5.2 – Sustainable Organizational Change

Managing Change Agents Skills

Every organization's change process, no matter how simple or complex, finds itself in situations where immediate change is required, and change agents are sough out to manage the process. Using one or more change agents is vital in smoothing the change process; it helps the organization simplify processes to generate efficiencies and improve productivity, implement large-scale organizational or systems change, and develop staff leadership ability to build environments that are open to change.

To be successful, change agents must posses a series of skill sets tailored for the changing environment. Figure 5.3 provides a list of the main skill sets a change agent should obtain and master. Notice that skills may vary when addressing change agents, teams and the system itself. Also notice that the change management system should encompass all the skills listed, while the individual professional or team may not need some of those skill sets.

Figure 5.3 – Change Agent's Skills

Change Agent Roles at the Professional Level

Change agents should be able to take existing inefficient, ineffective work and/or bureaucratic processes and improve them with fast and flawless implementation while producing significant cost savings and meeting other corporate goals. Such processes should be focused on helping "hands-on," cross functional teams, composed of people who are close to the actual work, identify ways of substantially simplifying processes and eliminating bureaucracy. At the end of the process, empowered decision-makers make "go" or "no go" decisions based on the team's recommendations. To reach this goal, change agents should use five basic steps:

o   Identify a planning team to define the problem.

o   Bring together representatives involved in the problem area for a highly structured and carefully crafted training program (1 to 3 day workshop).

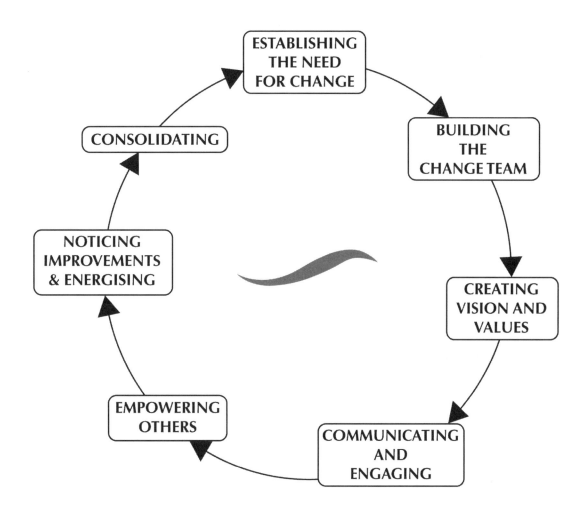

Figure 5.2

Related to			
Skills the Change Agents need to acquire	**Self**	**Team**	**System**
Technical Skills of the Specific Sector			X
Quality Management		X	X
Listening and Inquiry Skills		X	X
Defining Objectives / Visioning	X	X	X
Understanding Mental Maps / Shifting Perspectives	X	X	X
Resource Orientation	X	X	X
Dealing with Complexity	(X)	(X)	X
Learning from Mistakes / Feedback	X	X	X
Coaching		X	X
Leadership		X	X
Training Skills		X	X
Facilitation Skills		X	X
Large System Change Tools		(X)	X
Understanding and Catalysing Self-Organization		(X)	X

Table 1: Skills of Change Agents (X = strongly needed, (X) = partly needed)

Figure 5.3

o   Lead the teams in analyzing current processes and recommending changes that should be implemented in order to quickly bring about improvements.

o   Create a detailed plan for change.

o   Empower the teams to make their recommendations directly to the decision-makers who can authorize execution using state-of-the-art processes to ensure rapid results.

Change Agent Roles at the Team Level

Most organizations never lack a good change management plan. Rather, the problem more often than not is flawed execution. The role of teams as change agents in the change implementation process can be especially effective when:

o   Executing change involves large numbers of people in many locations

o   Dealing with organizations in which resistance to change is high

o   Working with organizations for whom cost saving potential—or the cost of not changing—is high.

Change agent teams should be capable of building internal implementation capacity and improving the organization's ability to execute complex, large-scale changes, as illustrated in Figure 5.4. Using various tools and methodologies, change agent teams should also be able to train change agents, and provide them and the organization with the necessary knowledge, skills, and processes to help employees proactively implement and manage strategic change initiatives (such as mergers, outsourcing, restructuring, quality/service improvements and new hardware/software installations and cultural change).

Figure 5.4 - Moving through the process of change

Change Agent Roles at the System Level

The main objective of a change agent system is to build change champions. The focus of the system is to lead change, by educating and supporting leaders/executives on the roles and responsibilities of being good leaders in times of turbulent change, particularly in organizations where change is needed across cultural and national borders.

A good change management system, which should be embedded and deployed as a change management office (CMO), should be able to help train leaders to become both sophisticated "buyers" of change and

Maintaining a Good Thing for Life!

Taking Action

Relapses
or sliding
backwards
occasionally
is not unusual

Not
Ready
Yet

Preparing for Action

Thinking about it

Figure 5.4

responsible "owners" and "champions" of the changes authorized. Training programs should focus on both individual and organizational assessments. Hence the organization's history of leadership success/failure, as well as its collective implementation skills, should be assessed prior to any change implementation taking place. The CMO should also provide individual leaders with skills that enhance their adaptability and talents in moving people away from the status quo.

Developing a Change Management Office

Developing a Change Management Office (CMO) begins with a solid management strategy. Often companies undergoing several business process changes or reengineering tend to focus on the more practical, result-oriented goals of their projects, but fail to assess the status, as a group, of their change management process. The result may be a cost savings in the short term, but a waste of time and resources (financial, human and intellectual capital) in the long run, often resulting in project failure.

The Need for Balance in Change Management Strategies

At MGCG, we believe that one of the most important roles of a leader is to put business and market strategies in place, and then influence and direct the business to ensure that goals and objectives are met. Trying to keep up with the constant pace of change makes this a tough challenge. For that reason, MGCG adopts and recommends a well-defined Change Management Strategy (CMS) focus, aimed at setting organizations on a winning game plan and the process of change.

The CMS strategy, based on our Knowledge Tornado methodology, enables leaders to anticipate the future, balance organic growth with acquisition growth, and put in place an effective strategic measurement system that provides a real time method to perceive organizational performance in the mist of change. A "one-size-fits-all" approach is not effective for change management. Think about these changes:

o   Acquiring a company of near or equal size

o   Getting suppliers to use a new web-based form and process

o   Implementing an Enterprise Resource Planning (ERP) solution

o   Releasing a new product

o   Relocating office spaces within an existing building

o   Reorienting around processes instead of functions

These are all distinctly different changes, but each requires change management to be successful. Each impacts people and how they do their job. Each can suffer from slow adoption and low utilization. Each has risks associated with people not becoming engaged or resisting the change.

It is therefore important that organizations invest some time and money in developing a change management strategy that is balanced and in line with its strengths, weaknesses, opportunities and threats (SWOT). Once leaders are aware of these important corporate attributes, and the change management strategy business elements, it is time to develop a change management office. This office should be put in charge of implementing and monitoring the changes in people and business processes.

A balanced change management strategy element includes:

o Situational awareness - understand the change and who is impacted

o Supporting structures - team and sponsor structures

o Strategy analysis - risks, resistance and special tactics

While each of these initiatives, in order to be successful, require change management, the right amount and approach for change management processes will vary depending on the results of the SWOT analysis. When done right, this analysis should provide a better understanding of the project at hand, with regards to human capital and teams, the primary motivation for change, how people will be directly impacted by the change, the degree in which project objectives are being met, the degree in which projects are on schedule, the level of sponsorship and management involvement, change management resource needs, and many other factors. The change management strategy should define the approach needed to manage change given the unique situation of the project or initiative.

How Change Management Offices Are Developed

The development of a CMO starts by establishing a sound situational awareness:

o Change characteristics - Begin by understanding the change that is being introduced. Changes can be formalized projects, strategic initiatives or even small adjustments to how the organization operates. Understanding the characteristics of the change requires you to answer questions like: What is the scope of the change? How many people will be impacted? Who is being impacted? Are the people being impacted the same or are they experiencing the change differently? What is being changed - processes, systems, job roles, etc? What is the timeframe for the change?

o Organizational attributes - Next, work to understand the people and groups being impacted by the change. Organizational attributes are related to the history and culture in the organization, and describe the backdrop against which this particular change is being introduced. What is the perceived need for this change among employees and managers? How have past changes been managed? Is there a shared vision for the organization? How much change is going on right now?

o Impacted groups - The final step in building the situational awareness is developing a map of who in the organization is being impacted by the change and how they are being impacted. A single change - say the deployment of a web-based expense reporting program - will impact different groups very differently. Employees that do not have expenses to report will not be impacted at all. Staffs that travel once a quarter will be only slightly impacted. Associates who are on the road all the time will be more impacted, although filing expenses is only a portion of their day-to-day work. And for those in accounting who manage expense reporting, their jobs will be completely altered. Outlining the impacted groups and showing how they will be impacted enables specific and customized plans later in the change management process.

Once that stage is complete, it is time now to understand and develop the CMO's supporting structure, which includes:

o Team structure - The change management team structure identifies who will be doing the change management work. It outlines the relationship between the project team and the change management team. The most frequent team structures include 1) change management being a responsibility assigned to one of the project team members or 2) an external change management team supporting a project team. The key in developing the strategy is to be specific and make an informed decision when assigning change management responsibility and resources.

o Sponsor coalition - The sponsor coalition describes the leaders and managers that need to be on-board for the change to be successful. Starting with the primary sponsor (the person who authorized and funded the change), the sponsor model documents the leaders of the groups that are being impacted by the change. The change characteristics will determine who must be part of the coalition. Each member of the sponsor coalition has the responsibility to build support and communicate the change with their respective audiences.

At this point, the CMO can then tackle one of its most important functions, which is to develop a strategic analysis and devise a balanced plan of action drawn from those analyses. These should include analysis of:

o Risk assessment - The risk of not managing the people side on a particular change is related to the dimensions described in the situational awareness section. Changes that are more dramatic and father reaching in the organization have a higher change management risk. Likewise, organizations and groups with histories and cultures that resist change face higher change management risk. In developing the strategy, overall risk and specific risk factors are documented.

o Anticipated resistance – After a project is introduced and meets resistance, members of the team often reflect that "they saw that reaction coming." In creating the change management strategy, identify where resistance can be expected. Are particular regions or divisions impacted differently than others? Were certain groups advocating a different solution to the same problem? Are some groups heavily invested in how things are done today? Note particular anticipated resistance points which can vary depending on how each group is related to the change.

o Special tactics - The final step of the change management strategy is the identification of any special tactics that will be required for this particular change initiative. These special tactics will delineate many of the lessons from the strategy development related to the change, and how the change will impact different groups in the organization. Throughout change implementation, special tactics may need to be revisited and updated.

Once the CMO formulates the change management strategy it will have completed the first critical step in implementing a change management methodology. The strategy provides direction and results in informed decision-making throughout the change process. A well-formulated strategy really brings the project or change to life, describing who and how it will impact the organization.

The change management strategy also contributes to the formulation of the rest of the change management plans. For instance, the groups identified in the strategy should each be addressed specifically in the communication plan. Steps for building and maintaining the coalition identified in the strategy are part of the sponsorship roadmap. Each subsequent change management plan and activity is guided by the findings in the change management strategy, as depicted in Figure 5.5.

Figure 5.5 – Balanced change management strategy

CMOs meet their objectives when they manage the human side of change effectively. A robust change management strategy sets the stage for effective and balanced change management and project success.

Change management strategy		Change management plans
• Situational awareness • Supporting structure • Strategy analysis	> *drives* >	• Communication plan • Sponsorship roadmap • Coaching plan • Training plan • Resistance management plan • Reinforcement planning

Figure 5.5

Chapter 6
Dealing with Resistance to Change

Any belief or value that has been previously successful in meeting needs will be resistant to change.

One of the primary sources of resistance to change is the organization's culture. CKOs and other KM professionals involved with organizational learning are typically well aware of this. But unless senior staff and leaders understand what organizational culture entails, very little can be accomplished in dealing with resistance to change. By definition, organizational culture is a pattern of common and shared basic assumptions that the organization has learned as it solved its problems of external adaptation and internal integration. Furthermore, it has worked well enough to be considered valid and, therefore, to be taught to new members as the correct way to perceive, think and feel in relation to those challenges. David Drennan[1] simply states it as *how things get done around here.*

When dealing with the need to change, to know who or what caused the need for change is important; not so important, however, if you look at it proactively, as illustrated in Figure 6.1. Of course, it is important to know who or what *moved your cheese,* so you can both run after it or them and compete to get it back. This is what I call a reactive approach to change, which does not necessarily lead to innovation, as chances are your cheese was moved as a result of innovation, only not generated by you or your organization. Thus you must move your cheese before someone does it for you, or as Jack Welch[2] once said, *change before you have to.*

Figure 6.1 – As Jack Welch, former CEO of GE once said: "change before you have to."

Successful change must lead to innovation. Otherwise your organization is only playing catch-up. Often, failed attempts to change are a result of lack of vision. In such cases you find plenty of plans and programs, but no vision. Success is result of a vision in action. If your organization is pursuing change based on a vision, but is not successful, verify your action plans, as very likely

---

[1] Transforming Company Culture, McGraw-Hill, New York, 1992.
[2] Excellence in Management & Leadership Series, Jack Welch, MICA Group, Canada, 2001

Figure 6.1

there is not much action in place. This is typically due to resistance or fear. By the same token, if you believe you have a good action plan and have the support of the organization, yet still you are not being successful in implementing changes (and consequently not innovating), you must check your vision, or lack thereof.

Always remember, innovative success is the result of vision in action. Some immediate actions that can be taken when managing change should include:

- Create a new vision

- Define a mission statement, core values, basic principles, and an operating style.

- Create a quality council of senior leaders to oversee the change process

Removing, Reshaping and Repositioning the Cheese

Organizations deal with change differently, depending on the stage they find themselves in. For that reason, the phenomenon in which knowledge managers whose organizational change project starts with great promise but fails to live up to that promise and eventually does not make the grade as successful reengineering, or plain change, is unfortunately more common than one would expect.

Creative individuals stand out from the rest of us, and often have odd reporting relationships. However, they somehow instinctively insert themselves into organizations wherever they are needed, and the changes and innovations they bring are often more like leaps than the small steps most of us experience. They think of the world in large terms, and their creativity comes from the novel connections they make between their work and their experience or observations. They are usually curious and need a field in which to exercise that curiosity. Leaders can work to bring the special and creative gifts of these people to bear on the efforts of a group.

CKOs and knowledge managers are catalysts in this process, as knowledge strategies enable organizations to enhance their business competencies, whether they are focused on efficient operations, product innovation or customer intimacy, thus becoming an important component of removing and reshaping the cheese. By capitalizing on knowledge, by strategically managing and acting on it, organizations can generate tremendous value for shareholders and customers.

In order for CKOs to become an effective instrument for change in organizations, they must attend to the fact that any organization in a growth stage has their leaders focusing on the development of group values and assumptions. Thus what leaders pay attention to, control and reward, as well as how they allocate resources, select, promote and eliminate people, is very important during this stage. This is a phase in the organization where there is a lot of personnel recasting, mission focusing and establishing of business processes. CKOs are even more important in the change process when the organization matures, as leaders begin to lose their ability to manipulate the organization, thus making it more difficult to enforce change. This is a very sensitive stage for any organization experiencing change, as earlier strengths can turn into liabilities, and often what leaders had believed to be an organization's weakness can very well become what was required of it as strength, in a different context.

Therefore I propose that organization leaders tap CKOs use of their KM skills, as well as their desirably eclectic backgrounds, to help them promote change in the organization. CKOs are the most adequate senior professional for the task, mainly because changing deeply held values and assumptions in any organization requires considerable effort, time, and understanding of human behavior and culture in organizations. Nonetheless, as discussed in chapter two, we need a new breed of CKO in order to be successful in the changing process. CKOs must posses two or three of the following characteristics, and must help their executive peers, in particular the CEO, to also posses as many as these traits as possible:

- Ambitious – Do people in your organization perceive you as someone that has managed your career well over the years? Do they have confidence that if they stick with you they too can benefit from your successes?

- Excellent motivator and team-builder – Are you a team leader? Do people easily follow your dreams and directions, despite your vision's lack of clarity at times? In other words, do people have faith in you? You should always be able to develop visions of the future that are relatively easy to communicate and appeal to customers, employees, and stockholders. There are times, however, when one must believe what cannot yet be seen.

- Loyal and of proactive management habits – Are you willing to make sacrifices for the organization and its members? Would you be willing to temporarily sacrifice your salary so that you could make ends meet in the organization? This is a trait a CEO must posses if she/he is to garner the respect and loyalty of the employees, especially in though times.

- Outgoing, well-liked, enchanting – Are you or your CEO a true enchanter, a person that people like to hang out with, listen to? Are you or your CEO seen as charming?

- Outstanding reputation – Do people in the organization perceive you and the CEO as someone with a high level of competence and potential for success?

- Survived organizational restructuring or change of management – Do you have a history of surviving corporate shakeouts, which may indicate an inherit value to the organization and an above-average emotional intelligence (EQ)?

- Technically savvy – Do you or your CEO have a reputation for being technically brilliant, insightful and visionary?

Having two or more of the traits listed above positions leaders for success in promoting change in their organization. However, as Edgar H. Schein[3] comments, leaders should be able to understand how culture is created, embedded, developed and ultimately manipulated, managed and changed. Many problems that were once viewed simply as communication failures or lack of teamwork are in essence a breakdown of intercultural communications. For instance, many companies today are trying to improve their designing and manufacturing processes, as well as the delivery of new products to customers.

---

[3] In Organizational Culture and Leadership, Jossey-Bass Business & Management Series, 1997.

However, the coordination of the marketing, engineering, manufacturing, distribution and sales groups requires more than the organization's willingness to change and improve. It also requires more than good intentions and a slew of management perks. Such a level of integration and proactive change requires a much better understanding of the subcultures of each of these functions, and the structure of the typical group interaction processes that allow communication and collaboration across sub-cultural boundaries. KM practices are key in this process, as KM professionals, in particular CKOs can develop the necessary cultural analysis to better understand how new technologies influence and are influenced by organizations.

In this context, a new technology tends to be a reflection of an occupational culture that is built around new core scientific concepts. CKOs would have the responsibility to develop cultural analyses for the executive staff across national and ethnic boundaries. Thus organizational learning, development and planned change cannot be understood without considering culture as a primary source of resistance to change. As Leonard-Barton asserts, in her book titled *Wellsprings of Knowledge: Building and Sustaining the Sources of Innovation,*[4] leaders must increase their study of culture and place the research on a solid conceptual foundation. She also alerts that superficial concepts of culture will not be useful. We must come to understand fully what culture is all about in human groups, organizations and nations, so that we can have a much deeper understanding of what goes on, why it goes on, and what, if anything, we can do about it.

Since cultural issues cannot be understood on the fly; changes in the organization can be very complex if conducted in a single, process-oriented fashion. Thus change must be conducted in a three-step approach, much similar to Spencer's model in his *Who Moved My Cheese* book: removing, reshaping and repositioning.

Removing the Cheese

Removing the cheese from the organization is the first step in seeking out changes and promoting innovation. The process of removing the cheese should be backed up with information or data showing negative trends or tendencies, proving that the current *cheese* is no longer healthy for the organization or its individuals. For instance, the organization is failing to meet some of its goals, or its systems are not working as efficiently as required.

Leaders, CKOs I would add, must make sure that this negative information is fully recognized and explicitly linked to important organizational goals, in order to produce a feeling of guilt or anxiety within the organization. Using the community of practice approach, peer-group discussions and other KM tools, leaders then must provide a new vision to serve as a psychological bridge from the current situation to the new one. Here again, bridging the knowledge gap created by changes in the environment or business landscape is very important. At this stage, CKOs must act very cautiously though, with much regard for the well being of the organization's members, much like dealing with a close relative that has just lost someone or something very close and dear to their hearts.

A leader connects creative people to the entire organization. A leader does not demand unreasonable personal or corporate loyalty, understanding that creative persons are loyal to an

---

[4] Harvard Business School Press, 1998, p169

idea and often appear to others as not so flexible. Their work rises from discovering and connecting. People remember the story of Archimedes' discovering the principle of displacement while taking a bath because it demonstrates that creative people have insights in all kinds of contexts. Art Fry realized the potential of Post-it notes while singing in his church choir. Hewlett-Packard began in a garage. Leaders understand the potential of connections like these and make it possible for creative persons to discover them.

The word *removing* can be a negative word in itself, pointing to a notion of loss, emptiness, void and despair. Thus it is here, at this first stage that most organizations give up on changing. At this point all the organization knows is that the current state of affairs is not healthy, no good and needs change, but it is part of human nature to resist change. Therefore, reshaping the cheese is a very important stage, one that will determine the success of failure of change in the organization, which the pure essence of innovation depends on. Quality programs must be developed during the reshaping stage to review:

- The establishment or refocus of mission statements and objectives

- The creation of a new strategic plan

- The development of quality councils, to assess and re-evaluate the quality of the staff in line with new missions and goals, thus preventing the miscast of staff, and determining individual and team training needs

- The development of process action teams and measurement indicators or metrics.

- The development of individual and team quality award programs to be implemented during the repositioning of the cheese.

Also, during the removing of the cheese, make sure to include training as one of the basic thrusts of quality programs. Training courses and workshops ranging from awareness, team member and team leader programs to customer satisfaction, teamwork skills and continuous process improvement programs, should all be included.

The organization's and employee's visions, missions, credos and core values serve as cultural embedding mechanisms. Thus it is important that throughout the change project leaders continuously refer to, and reinforce, management actions by providing directions to guide action and change. A good idea is to develop frames and small posters to be affixed on the walls of the organization, as a constant reminder to employees that they are all engaged in the changing process. It is when these espoused concepts and values are continually reinforced and discussed that the organization and its employees begin to move deeper into the new culture, thus impacting the basic values and shared assumptions of the group. This takes conscious commitment over time.

The concept of commitment during the removing and reshaping of the cheese is also very important, as commitment at all levels is critical to institutionalizing change. If overlooked, lack of commitment turns into resistance. Commitment can also be lost when employees see leadership not walking the talk, which includes but is not limited to:

- Canceling staff and quality council meetings or continually sending replacement attendees

- Demanding unrealistic leaps in productivity over short periods of time

- Continually overriding team recommendations

- Forcing change, or not enforcing it at all

- When the excitement and fervor of the new initiative quickly wares off.

Reshaping the Cheese

With the organization's current (or obsolete) knowledge system *removed*, leaders now must think about restructuring the organization's basic assumptions, the employees' basic believe system and their basic knowledge base. Leaders now must reshape the organization's cheese! This restructuring process, chaotic by nature, is what I called the *eye of the knowledge tornado* earlier on in this book. As the organization attempts to move out of the eye, the chaos, it begins to develop a new, and often adjusted, set of basic assumptions, as well as a change in behavior, as illustrated in Figure 6.2.

Figure 6.2 - In face of constant change, leaders now must reshape the organization's cheese!

At this stage, a clear vision of what the organization wants to achieve is very important. Without one, the changing effort can easily dissolve into a very confusing project, with many incompatible initiatives, which can take the organization in a completely different and dangerously wrong direction. Furthermore, the onset of a blurry vision will produce lack of cooperation from the individuals in the organization, who will not be willing to make any sacrifices, especially if they are unhappy with the status quo. At this stage everyone must believe that useful and fruitful change is possible. Thus credible communication, consistently delivered, is a must if leaders want to capture the hearts and minds of the organization as a whole. More than ever, at this stage, success will be the result of vision in action.

CKOs can be very effective here by using gentle and consistently applied pressure on the organization regarding the vision, the actions to take the organization there, and the rewards that awaits once they get there. Some strategies may include:

- Lively articles about the new vision, delivered through the organization's newsletter. If you don't have one, create one!

- Replace the boring and ritualistic weekly staff meetings with exciting discussions on the changes being undertaken

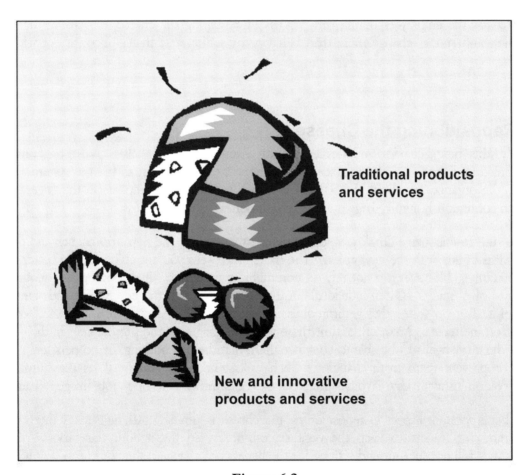

Traditional products and services

New and innovative products and services

Figure 6.2

- Make change the core objective of the organization. For instance, instead of discussing sales pipelines, discuss what needs to change this week so that the organization can be more profitable. Instead of discussing performance planning and reviews, discuss how individuals in the organization can obsolete themselves on a daily basis, in all fronts.

- Most importantly, talk about how everyone in the organization, beginning with the CEO and the executive staff, can walk the talk. How can everyone consciously attempt to become a living symbol of the organization's new culture?

Keep in mind that communication comes in both words and deeds, and the latter are often the most powerful and effective form. Be careful with leadership behavior, as well as the posture adopted by the employees during this process of reshaping the cheese, refocusing the vision. Nothing undermines change more than behavior by senior staff that is inconsistent with their words.

Repositioning the Cheese

Finally, this new behavior and desired set of assumptions and beliefs must be continually reinforced until there is no more anxiety throughout the organization and in the system. At this point, the organization should be stabilized. Thus, to successfully reposition the cheese, make sure to continuously involve large numbers of supporters as you progress.

Make sure to encourage employees, emboldening them to try the new approaches and develop new ideas in line with the new vision. The more employees you get involved, the better will be the outcome. However, do not rely on communication alone. Repositioning also requires the removal of obstacles. Often individuals in the organization see the new vision and want to be part of it. But very often they get immobilized by a wall that appears in front of them, rendering the effort ineffective. Most of the time these walls are imaginary and present only in their minds. Thus the challenge is to be able to convince them that there is nothing, or no personal risks, to stop or prevent them from changing. Such walls tend to be very real, as the human self-preservation instinct tries to avoid actions that can be detrimental to one's job, image or career.

Another important aspect in repositioning the cheese is timing. Change takes time, so it is important for leaders to keep the organization motivated throughout the process. Most employees will not stick around waiting for the benefits of change if they need too wait too long. Thus make sure to plan for at least some small results within 12 to 24 months. Without these short-term results, employees might begin to give up on the vision, and even display resistance to the changes.

CKOs again bring an advantage to the change process as leaders are pressured to produce short-term results. Since CKOs typically are not so involved with the management of employees and their everyday responsibilities of keeping up with business processes, they fit very well in the role of *bad cop*. Direct managers do not like the fact that they may be forced to produce short-term results for the changes taking place. At this stage, pressure can be very useful in achieving this goal, particularly because once managers and employees realize that major changes will be slower to materialize, the urgency level tends to drop. By not being directly in the line of fire, CKOs can help to keep the urgency level up, while promoting business intelligence activity that may enable the clarification or revision of the vision.

Finally, a successful repositioning of the cheese or a successful change in the organization is measured by how well the changes become embedded in the organization's new culture, seeped into the way its employees conduct their everyday business. As discussed earlier, an organization's culture can be summarized by the way things are done. By the same token, a successful change would have been institutionalized throughout the organization, and would now become part of its culture.

To ensure changes are institutionalized in the organization's culture, knowledge about the change and the new of doing things has to be turned into action. One way of verifying that is by consciously attempting to show employees all the positive results the new approach, behavior and attitude have brought to the organization and its performance. It is very important that leaders make an effort to communicate such accomplishments, as employees may not realize it by themselves or, even worse, may establish very inaccurate view of the results.

For instance, at Virtual Access Networks, I was once asked to manage the research group working on a new wireless technology concept that had failed under previous management. This was an unusual situation for a CKO to be in, but I believe management understood that most of the challenges the group faced were not of a technical nature, but of a multicultural and motivational one. It was clear that several changes had to take place in that group if it wanted to be successful, which was not a choice.

As I began removing the cheese, the team character of the members began to clash with the new vision. At one point half of the group even threatened to resign if they were forced to change. But after much communication, group lunches, peer-quality reinforcement meetings and the development of a unique identity, the group finally began to turn around, accepting the new shape of the cheese. We were finally able to successfully reposition the group, its goals and deliverables in record time. However, the group did not naturally take ownership of their success, and few even expressed that the reason they stayed around was in consideration to me. These team members at first clearly missed the point, as there is no way that one person alone can change a group unless each element of the group does their part, beginning by believing in the new vision and doing their best to succeed. It was necessary for us to meet as a group and individually few times in order to emphasize that the glory for the accomplishment was theirs, both individually and as a group, and not their leader's alone.

The group today is self-sufficient and successfully operates under that new vision. Furthermore, at least one successor rose up from the pack and is ready to lead that group. Leaders must breed new leaders.

Closing the Circle of Innovation: Forget the Cheese!

In the knowledge economy, innovation is not only a necessity, it is king. Unless a learning organization gains access to new ideas that in turn can help the generation of innovation, timely dialogue cannot be established, promising ideas cannot be disseminated. But conducting business at the speed of thought gets more complicated than this, as different industries operate at different levels of change and thus need to use different approaches to succeed.

The goal of every innovator should be two-fold; first, to forget about the cheese they have or use to have. Such cheese, be it a technology, skill set, customer base, current product or service, has been moved by market forces, competition, obsolescence or economic shifts. Thus, the challenge now is to forget the cheese and, secondly, focus on creating a new one, which will require more than simply chasing the cheese or responding to its demand. Think about some of the many times cheeses were moved in the past few decades:

- Chrysler moved the automobile industry's cheese in 1993 with the introduction of the minivan. At that time, a van mounted on a car chassis with folding seats and cup-holders moved the cheese of every automaker, as well as car buyers.

- Sony moved its customers' and the industry's cheese when it told them to strap its music players around their head, giving birth to Walkmans.

- Napster moved the cheese of record label companies when it forced them to adapt to a new way of distributing and selling music tracks over the Internet.

- Audible is moving the cheese of hardcopy book sellers and readers by making it available over the internet on MP3 format, allowing people to enjoy a book even if they are driving, flying or jogging, with the lights off in bed or in group.

In this new economy, successful companies are not those capable of surviving the move of their cheese, which is very important, but those capable of letting their cheese go so that they can search for more enjoyable and gratifying cheese. Thus innovation is the main ingredient to spark new sources of revenue based on changing and disruptive technologies, demographics, and consumer habits. Just like a new kind of cheese can destroy the demand of old ones, new business models can also destroy old ones.

Therefore, moving the cheese to promote innovation is a threat to every traditional, uninspired business. Never before have strategy life cycles been shorter and market leadership counted for less. If you or your company is not pursuing innovation, rest assured that it will only be a matter of time before you become overwhelmed by it. Strategic innovation is the only way to deal with discontinuous -- and disruptive -- change.

Demystifying Innovation

Innovation is not something that can be predicted or scheduled. Thus existing orthodoxies and obsolete business models must be revised, if not let go all together, if innovation is to be promoted. True and insightful innovation demonstrates that prompt new ideas are never bound to predictability, or to corporate brownbag and strategic meetings calendars.

One of Nokia's most successful cellular phones, the rainbow-hued phone, emerged from an afternoon at the beach in California, and not out of a strategic meeting in an air-conditioned think tank room at the company's head quarters. The innovation also gave birth to the inspiration that would further Nokia's success with cellular phones: mobile phones are not only a communication tool, but also a fashion accessory. But very few companies follow Nokia steps, especially in the United States, where a hierarchy of organizations dominates a hierarchy of ideas. Innovation can only be fostered if the encouragement for new ideas is unlocked across the organization. One way of doing this is by bringing together a cross-section of employees, at all levels and groups of the organization, to share their ideas and any new perspectives that may contain the kernel of a fruitful and even market-disruptive new idea.

Developing an Innovation Paradigm

The process of innovation cannot be anticipated or predicted, but it can be consciously developed, as long as learning organizations are willing to dump the cheese that is preventing them from being innovative, such as old policies, procedures, cultures and habits, and upend cherished conventions. As a rule of thumb, past achievement imposes resistance against future adaptability by developing policies and subtle ways of doing things that cause the organization to undermine and even totally ignore innovative insights.

Therefore, one of the major threats for organizations in the ever-evolving knowledge economy is their past successes. The laser focus of the past becomes the set of blinders of today, lessening an organization's ability to discern what is truly new and what is already known. Glimmers of great ideas are evident in most organizations. However people, from upper management on down, tend to be resistant to change, and will tend to target those new ideas as a foreign variable to the organization's culture or know-how. Thus instead of welcoming new insights, most organizations attack those ideas as foreign enemies threatening the status quo of their organization.

In the United Kingdom, for example, where knowledge management and innovation are seen as catalysts to a competitive edge, some organizations are capitalizing on the shift of an innovation paradigm. Richard Branson, CEO of Virgin Enterprises, encourages every one of his employees to call him and share a new idea. They all have his cellular phone number. A successful example of his strategy is the wedding planning boutique Virgin Bride, which resulted from one of Branson's Virgin flight attendants having problems in planning her own wedding. She called Branson and the boutique was created. In the United States, however, seldom you will find a CEO that is willing to share his cellular number with his employees. Believe me, I have tested it, and as a senior staff member!

In developing an innovation paradigm, you must also institutionalize innovation by building a safe place for people to think new thoughts. In some companies, new ideas are in short supply, muffled by an organizational climate that deprives the intellectual oxygen, discourages change, and demands conformity. An innovation paradigm should promote the plentiful generation of ideas, and then make sure that those ideas can be turned into action. More precisely, ideas generate new knowledge, new know-how, which is not worth anything unless your organization knows how-to convert this knowledge into action.

Chapter 7
Embracing Change Management

Successful change initiatives require strong, committed leadership throughout the entire project life-cycle.

Every business executive I meet has always had a simple goal for themselves and their organizations: stability. Shareholders want little more than predictable earnings growth. In the past, because so many markets were either closed or undeveloped, leaders could deliver on those expectations through annual exercises that offered only modest modifications to the strategic plan. Prices stayed in check; people stayed in their jobs; life was good.

As discussed thought this book, market transparency, labor mobility, global capital flows and instantaneous communication have blown that comfortable scenario to smithereens. In most industries — and in almost all companies, from giants on down — heightened global competition has concentrated management's collective mind on something that, in the past, it happily avoided: change.

This presents most executives with an unfamiliar and very uncomfortable challenge. As large organizations undergo major transformations, they and their advisors conventionally focus their attention on devising the best strategic and tactical plans. But to succeed, they must also have an intimate understanding of the human side of change management— the alignment of the company's culture, values, people and behaviors— to encourage the desired results. Plans themselves do not capture value; value is realized only through the sustained, collective actions of the thousands— perhaps the tens of thousands— of employees who are responsible for designing, executing and living with the changed environment.

The challenge is that any long-term structural change has four characteristics that are often misunderstood:

- Scale - the change affects all or most of the organization

- Magnitude - it involves significant alterations to the status quo

- Duration - it lasts for months, if not years

- Strategic importance.

Many senior executives know this and worry about it. In a survey conducted by the magazine Strategy+Business in 2004, when asked what kept them up at night, CEOs involved in transformation often said they were concerned about how the work force would react, how they could get their team to work together, and how they would be able to lead their people. They also worried about retaining their company's unique values and sense of identity, and about creating a culture of commitment and performance. Leadership teams that fail to plan for the human side of change often find themselves wondering why their best-laid plans have gone awry.

No single methodology fits every company, but there is a set of practices, tools and techniques that can be adapted to a variety of situations, addressing all aspects of the change management process, as depicted in Figure 7.1. The following is a list of guiding principles for change management. Using these as a systematic, comprehensive framework, you should be able to understand what to expect, how to manage your own personal change, and how to engage the entire organization in the process. The following recommendations first appeared in my KM book titled *The Knowledge Tornado*[1]:

Figure 7.1 – The Elements of Continuous Change Management

1. Address the "human side," the people who retain the knowledge, systematically. Any significant transformation creates "people issues." New leaders will be asked to step up, jobs will be changed, new skills and capabilities must be developed, and employees will be uncertain and resistant.

   Dealing with these issues on a reactive, case-by-case basis puts speed, morale and results at risk. A formal approach for managing change — beginning with the leadership team and then engaging key stakeholders and leaders — should be developed early and adapted often as change moves through the organization. This demands as much data collection and analysis, planning, and implementation discipline as it does a redesign of strategy, systems, or processes.

   The change-management approach should be fully integrated into program design and decision-making, both informing and enabling strategic direction. It should be based on a realistic assessment of the organization's history, readiness and capacity to change.

2. Start at the top. Because change is inherently unsettling for people at all levels of an organization, when it is on the horizon, all eyes will turn to the CEO and the leadership team for strength, support, and direction. The leaders themselves must embrace the new approaches first, both to challenge and to motivate the rest of the institution. They must speak with one voice and model the desired behaviors. The executive team also needs to

---

[1] Blackhall Publishing, 2002

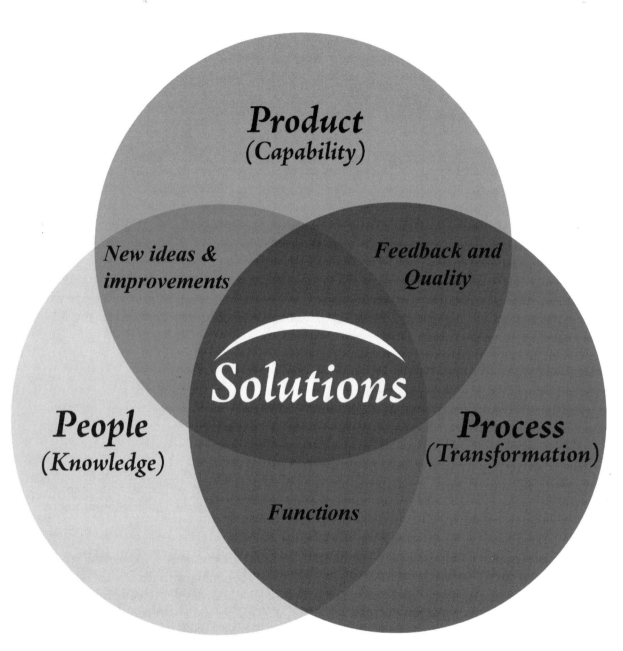

Figure 7.1

78

understand that, although its public face may be one of unity, it, too, is composed of individuals who are going through stressful times and need to be supported.

Executive teams that work well together are best positioned for success. They are aligned and committed to the direction of change, understand the culture and behaviors the changes intend to introduce, and can model those changes themselves. At one large transportation company, the senior team rolled out an initiative to improve the efficiency and performance of its corporate and field staff before addressing change issues at the officer level. The initiative realized initial cost savings but stalled as employees began to question the leadership team's vision and commitment. Only after the leadership team went through the process of aligning and committing to the change initiative was the work force able to deliver downstream results.

3. Involve every layer. As transformation programs progress from defining strategy and setting targets to design and implementation, they affect different levels of the organization. Change efforts must include plans for identifying leaders throughout the company and pushing responsibility for design and implementation down, so that change "cascades" through the organization. At each layer of the organization, the leaders who are identified and trained must be aligned to the company's vision, equipped to execute their specific mission, and motivated to make change happen.

    One of our clients, a major power generation company with consistently flat earnings, decided to change performance and behavior. The company followed this "cascading leadership" methodology, training and supporting teams at each stage. First, 15 officers set the strategy, vision, and targets. Next, more than 50 senior executives and managers designed the core of the change initiative. Then 350 leaders from the field drove implementation. The structure remained in place throughout the change program, which doubled the company's earnings far ahead of schedule. This approach is also a superb way for a company to identify its next generation of leadership.

4. Make the formal case. Individuals are inherently rational and will question to what extent change is needed, whether the company is headed in the right direction, and whether they want to commit personally to making change happen. They will look to the leadership for answers. The articulation of a formal case for change and the creation of a written vision statement are invaluable opportunities to create or compel leadership-team alignment.

    Three steps should be followed in developing the case:

    - First, confront reality and articulate a convincing need for change.

    - Second, demonstrate faith that the company has a viable future and the leadership to get there.

    - Third, provide a road map to guide behavior and decision-making. Leaders must then customize this message for various internal audiences, describing the pending change in terms that matter to the individuals.

A major pulp and paper company experiencing years of steadily declining earnings determined that it needed to significantly restructure its operations — instituting, among other things, a 30 percent work force reduction — to remain competitive. In a series of offsite meetings, the executive team built a brutally honest business case that downsizing was the only way to keep the business viable, and drew on the company's proud heritage to craft a compelling vision to lead the company forward. By confronting reality and helping employees understand the necessity for change, leaders were able to motivate the organization to follow the new direction in the midst of the largest downsizing in the company's history. Instead of being shell-shocked and demoralized, those who stayed felt a renewed resolve to help the enterprise advance.

5. Create ownership. Leaders of large change programs must overperform during the transformation and be the zealots who create a critical mass among the work force in favor of change. This requires more than mere buy-in or passive agreement that the direction of change is acceptable. It demands ownership by leaders willing to accept responsibility for making change happen in all of the areas they influence or control. Ownership is often best created by involving people in identifying problems and crafting solutions. It is reinforced by incentives and rewards. These can be tangible (for example, financial compensation) or psychological (for example, camaraderie and a sense of shared destiny).

    At a software development start-up that was getting ready to go public, the first department to create detailed designs for the new organization was human resources. Its personnel worked with advisors in cross-functional teams for more than six months. But as the designs were being finalized, top departmental executives began to resist the move to implementation. While agreeing that the work was top-notch, the executives realized they hadn't invested enough individual time in the design process to feel the ownership required to begin implementation. On the basis of their feedback, the process was modified to include a "deep dive." The departmental executives worked with the design teams to learn more, and get further exposure to changes that would occur. This was the turning point; and the transition then happened quickly. It also created a forum for top executives to work as a team, creating a sense of alignment and unity that the group hadn't felt before.

6. Communicate the message. Too often, change leaders make the mistake of believing that others understand the issues, feel the need to change and see the new direction as clearly as they do. The best change programs reinforce core messages through regular, timely advice that is both inspirational and practicable. Communication flows in from the bottom and out from the top, and is targeted to provide employees the right information at the right time, and to solicit their input and feedback. Often this will require over communication through multiple, redundant channels.

    In the late 1990s, the commissioner of the Internal Revenue Service, Charles O. Rossotti, had a vision: The IRS could treat taxpayers as customers and turn a feared bureaucracy into a world-class service organization. Getting more than 100,000 employees to think and act differently required more than just systems redesign and process change. IRS leadership designed and executed an ambitious communications program including daily voice mails from the Commissioner and his top staff, training sessions, videotapes, newsletters, and town hall meetings that continued through the transformation. Timely, constant, practical communication was at the heart of the program, which brought the IRS's customer ratings from the lowest in various surveys to its current ranking above the likes of McDonald's and most airlines.

7. Assess the cultural landscape. Successful change programs pick up speed and intensity as they cascade down, making it critically important that leaders understand and account for culture and behaviors at each level of the organization. Companies often make the mistake of assessing culture either too late or not at all. Thorough cultural diagnostics can assess organizational readiness to change, bring major problems to the surface, identify conflicts, and define factors that can recognize and influence sources of leadership and resistance. These diagnostics identify the core values, beliefs, behaviors and perceptions that must be taken into account for successful change to occur. They serve as the common baseline for designing essential change elements, such as the new corporate vision, and building the infrastructure and programs needed to drive change.

8. Address culture explicitly. Once the culture is understood, it should be addressed as thoroughly as any other area in a change program. Leaders should be explicit about the culture and underlying behaviors that will best support the new way of doing business, and find opportunities to model and reward those behaviors. This requires developing a baseline, defining an explicit end-state or desired culture, and devising detailed plans to make the transition.

Company culture is an amalgam of shared history, explicit values and beliefs, and common attitudes and behaviors. Change programs can involve creating a culture (in new companies or those built through multiple acquisitions), combining cultures (in mergers or acquisitions of large companies), or reinforcing cultures (in, say, long-established consumer goods or manufacturing companies). Understanding that all companies have a cultural center — the locus of thought, activity, influence or personal identification — is often an effective way to jump-start culture change.

A consumer goods company with a suite of premium brands determined that business realities demanded a greater focus on profitability and bottom-line accountability. In addition to redesigning metrics and incentives, it developed a plan to systematically change the company's culture, beginning with marketing, the company's historical center. It brought the marketing staff into the process early to create enthusiasts for the new philosophy who adapted marketing campaigns, spending plans and incentive programs to be more accountable. Seeing these culture leaders grab onto the new program, the rest of the company quickly fell in line.

9. Prepare for the unexpected. No change program goes completely according to plan. People react in unexpected ways; areas of anticipated resistance fall away; and the external environment shifts. Effectively managing change requires continual reassessment of its impact, and the organization's willingness and ability to adopt the next wave of transformation. Fed by real data from the field and supported by information and solid decision-making processes, change leaders can then make the adjustments necessary to maintain momentum and drive results.

A leading U.S. health-care company was facing competitive and financial pressures from its inability to react to changes in the marketplace. A diagnosis revealed shortcomings in its organizational structure and governance, and the company decided to implement a new operating model. In the midst of detailed design, a new CEO and leadership team took over. The new team was initially skeptical, but was ultimately convinced that a solid case for change, grounded in facts and supported by the organization at large, existed. Some adjustments were made to the speed and sequence of implementation, but the fundamentals of the new operating model remained unchanged.

10. Speak to the individual. Change is both an institutional journey and a very personal one. People spend many hours each week at work; many think of their colleagues as a second family. Individuals (or teams of individuals) need to know how their work will change, what is expected of them during and after the change program, how they will be measured, and what success or failure will mean for them and those around them. Team leaders should be as honest and explicit as possible. People will react to what they see and hear around them, and need to be involved in the change process. Highly visible rewards, such as promotion, recognition and bonuses, should be provided as dramatic reinforcement for embracing change. Sanction or removal of people standing in the way of change will reinforce the institution's commitment.

Most leaders contemplating change know that people matter. It is all too tempting, however, to dwell on the plans and processes, which don't talk back and don't respond emotionally, rather than face up to the more difficult and more critical human issues. But mastering the "soft" side of change management needn't be a mystery.

Chapter 8
Using GE's Change
Acceleration Process

Successful change initiatives require strong, committed leadership throughout the entire project life-cycle.

When Jack Welch, former CEO of General Electric, one day realized that GE needed to improve its ability to adapt to change so it could continue to be successful, he also realized that, like most companies, the challenge was not in managing the technical portion of change, but in accepting and managing change. He and his team also found that the majority of change initiatives didn't succeed, or under-performed, due to poor acceptance of the people leading change and/or those affected by it.

GE was able to identify a very distinct pattern where change, no matter if good or bad, with a strong technical plan, had poor results or failed when combined with a low acceptance component. They also found that changes with an average or low technical plan coupled with high acceptance from its constituents outperformed change initiatives with a high quality technical plan accompanied with a low acceptance plan consistently. It was under these premises that GE's Change Acceleration Process (CAP) was developed[1].

CAP is based on one simple equation: $E = Q \times A$ where:

- E represents the "effectiveness" of the result.

- Q is the "quality" (technical strategy) of the initiative.

- A is the "acceptance" (cultural strategy) of the initiative.

Resistance to change, as discussed in chapters three and six, can be high and in high places, in any company, any industry. Pockets of resistance can be found within any organization – a phenomenon that prompted GE to commission the development of the CAP model. As depicted in Figure 8.1, the quality, or "Q," yields effective results only if the focus on the

---

[1] General Electric / CAP materials presented at Michael Hammer seminar: Marketing Change: Selling Change to Internal Constituencies, presented by Kimberly-Clark. October 2001.

acceptance of change (the "A") is in place. This is represented by GE as "Q x A = E," where "E" is effective results.

Figure 8.1 – Helping Change Happen

The equation is key for any successful change initiative, where *quality* of the change initiative multiplied by the *acceptance* of the people involved in the change process, will result in the effectiveness of the effort. The emphasis here is in paying as much attention to the cultural aspects of the strategy as you would to the technical aspects. The process is based on seven stages aimed at the development of an efficient and effective change strategy as shown in Figure 8.2. They are:

- **Leading Change** – Sponsorship for the change is clear. Leaders publicly and privately commit to making change happen by garnering resources necessary to sustain it and by giving personal time and attention needed to follow through.

- **Creating a Shared Need** – The reason to change, whether driven by threat or opportunity, is widely shared through data, demonstration or diagnosis. The need for change must exceed its resistance.

- **Shaping a Vision** – The desired outcome of change is clear, legitimate, widely understood and shared.

- **Mobilizing Commitment** – There is a strong commitment from key stakeholders to engage in the change, make it work, and to demand and receive management attention. Responsibilities are established, and employees involved actively support progress through personal time, attention and learning.

- **Making Change Last** – Once change is started, it endures through implementation plans, follow-through and establishment of accountability. New learning is transferred throughout the organization.

- **Monitoring Progress** – Indicators are in place to monitor and measure progress; milestones are established and reached; benchmarks are set and realized.

- **Changing Systems & Structures** – This includes staffing, development, measurements and rewards, effective communication, organization design, information systems, and resource allocation systems.

Figure 8.2 – CAP Leading Change Process

Successful Change
(Lessons from IPCP)

$$Q \times A = E$$

"Q" (Quality) is the Technical Strategy

"A" (Acceptance) is the People Strategy

"E" (Effectiveness) is Sustained Change

Figure 8.1

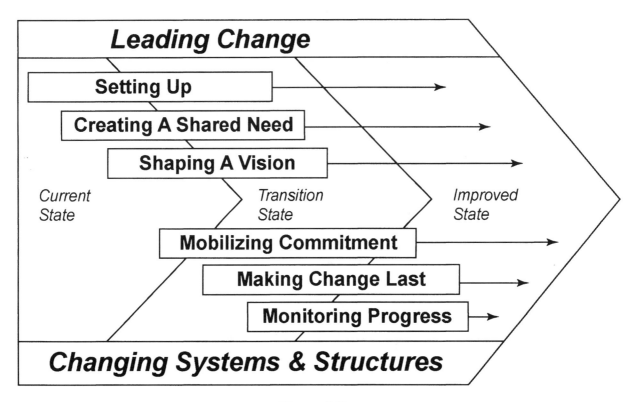

Figure 8.2

86

Note that successful change initiatives require strong, committed leadership throughout the entire project life-cycle. Strong and committed leadership is critical to accelerating change, as leadership impacts all other change processes. Therefore, change management implementations using CAP will require that leaders play varied roles. It will require:

- A willingness to take personal initiative and challenge the status quo.

- High levels of attention to the project through the time, passion and focus given to the project by leaders at all levels.

- Visible, active, and public commitment and support.

Does CAP Impact the Bottom Line?

As a change-management strategy, CAP combines a structured process with a robust set of tools to transform how people feel, operate and behave in an organization. Viewed by many as common sense, the CAP approach is seldom considered common practice. To succeed, it must be integrated into internal operating mechanisms and become part of the way in which an organization works.

At GE Plastics Japan there was nothing but red ink from 1989 to 1993. Managers signed up for CAP training as a last resort in 1994. By the end of the year the business was breaking even. In 1995 net income was $18 million and the company was on solid footing for the first time.

CAP works and impacts the bottom line because it is different from other change management initiatives in:

- **Structure**: CAP has a methodical structure, referred to as the CAP Model, enabling the trained Change Agent (CA) to determine which tool would produce the greatest outcome at each phase of the process.

- **Timing**: Change management programs often seek stakeholder buy-in after a change has been determined and implemented. CAP is used concurrently to head off resistance by factoring in stakeholder issues before change is determined and in place.

- **Toolset**: While other initiatives also provide an array of tools, they generally lack a framework within which participants are coached to operate. This may limit the effectiveness and appropriate use of the tools.

Some of the keys to CAP success include:

- Aligning CAP with management strategies to reinforce change

- Developing solid, consistent plans for communication

- Devoting time and resources to changing systems and structures

- Documenting sustainable implementation plans

- Driving leadership awareness and strategic support for the initiative

- Instilling effective tracking and accountability mechanisms

- Linking the CA role of CAP coaches to performance review

- Providing a 360° view: positive/negative, top/bottom, internal/external

As discussed earlier in this chapter, CAP focuses on the people side of change, complementing the technical strategy with human strategy. Think of it as an intellectual investment in your people to make them productive. That's why, when deploying it, CAP is best introduced at the executive level, where concepts and strategies are explained and embraced. It is at this point that plans are made as to how many CA should be trained, where to focus first and what the phased approach may look like in terms of the spread and depth of CAP deployment. Answers to these questions depend largely upon the size and objectives of the organization.

Selecting the Change Agents for CAP Implementations

Leadership should prepare for a high level of enthusiasm stemming from the first few CAP sessions. Because of this, it is often recommend that each service line become involved in training so CA are evenly distributed without bombarding one or two departments for facilitation needs.

Also, it is very important that the initial team of CA remain always networked – sharing best practices and lessons learned in a brief team meeting each month. CA should be paired for the first few assignments and develop a competency model that advances them to the solo facilitation level within a specific time frame. Also, since CAP is built on change and the need to improve, evaluations should be elicited from both peers (fellow Change Agents) and session participants.

The criteria for CAP coach selection should include:

- A professional that is considered one of your organization's "best and brightest"

- Demonstrated leadership capabilities (but not necessarily management level)

- Experienced facilitator comfortable with public speaking

- Individual interested in change management

- Strong interpersonal skills combined with a passion and desire to become a coach

- Well respected by others in your organization so people will listen to what he or she has to say

Developing a Successful CAP Subject/Session

Any change in your organization may be met with resistance. Any issue that is creating interpersonal issues – perhaps involving a misalignment of initiatives – would be ideal subject matter for a CAP session. As long as you have a trained facilitator, key stakeholders and a change-management initiative – whether departmental or organizational – the CAP model and its accompanying toolset will help to ensure success. Also, keep in mind, as depicted in Figure 8.3, the twelve principles for managing change.

Figure 8.3 – The Twelve Principles for Managing Change

These sessions should provide you and your professionals with a useful metaphor for change, and provide a practical set of perspectives for considering the strategic, cultural, and structural and resource parameters for change. In every company, these have specific applications and nuances. When companies attempt significant change initiatives without some level of "political, marketing and military" cross-preparation, they're in trouble from the start.

Figure 8.4 provides a summary of the tools and techniques used by CAP in the change process. I'd recommend you pick up some of the many books on CAP for more detailed information. Also, it is very important that effective change leadership be built rapidly and sustained throughout the entire change initiative. Keep in mind that CAP teams can potentially derail when they:

- Fail to engage and commit to behaviors necessary for change.

- Are transferred too quickly, before change has occurred.

- Try to do it all by themselves, without involving others.

- Shift to other goals and objectives, before completing the change initiative.

- Fail to establish, and clarify, the key change roles of Sponsor, Agent, Target and Champion.

- Allow the change process to be diluted by too many competing initiatives and priorities.

Figure 8.4 – Tools and Techniques for CAP Implementation

1. Thought processes and relationship dynamics are fundamental if change is to be sucessful.	2. Change only happens when each person makes a desicion to implement the change.
3. People fear change if "happens" to them.	4. Given the freedom to do so, people will build quality into their work as a matter of personal pride.
5. Traditional organizational systems treat people like children and expect them to act like adults.	6. "Truth" is more important during periods of change and uncertainty than "good news."
7. Trust is earned by those who demonstrate consistent behavior and clearly defined values.	8. People who work are capable of doing much more than they are doing.
9. The intrinsic rewards of a project are often more important than the material rewards and recoginition.	10. A clearly defined vision of the end result enables all the people to define the most efficient path for accomplishing the results.
11. The more input people have into defining the changes that will affect their work, the more they will take ownership for the results.	12. To change the individual, change the system.

Figure 8.3

Tactics & Tools Include:		Used For:
Model for Leading Change	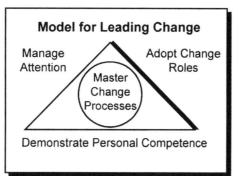	Illustrating the four inter-related elements of effective change leadership

Figure 8.4

The GE CAP method calls for collecting large teams of employees to define tough business decisions, then breaking into smaller teams to develop solutions. The small teams then meet with a manager in a "town meeting" to discuss their recommendations. The result is change that's brought about by employees themselves. A leading change personal auditing tool, as suggested in Figure 8.5, can be very useful in this process.

Figure 8.5 – Leading Change Personal Auditing

At its core, CAP is a simple, straightforward concept for cutting out bureaucracy and solving organizational problems - fast. Large groups of employees and managers - from different levels and functions of the organization - come together to address issues that they identify or that senior management has risen as concerns. In small teams, people challenge prevailing assumptions about "the way we've always done things" and come up with recommendations for dramatic improvements in organizational processes.

The CAP teams present their recommendations to a senior manager in a "town meeting", where the manager engages the entire group in a dialogue about the recommendations and then makes yes-or-no decisions on the spot. Recommendations for changing the organization are assigned to "owners" who have volunteered to carry them out and follow through to get results.

CAP can be applied to almost any type of problem and industry. It was first used at GE to harvest the low-hanging fruit of overgrown bureaucracy by getting unnecessary and unproductive work out of the organizational system - e.g. reduce meetings, reports, and approval levels. They asked what procedures didn't make sense, where time was being wasted, what activities seemed to add little value to the organization and so on.

In the core functions, bureaucracy is always found: filling out forms for deals, preparing presentations for approval meetings, keeping track of customer data, obtaining approval for materials purchasing, overwhelming amounts of extra analysis to justify various investments or initiatives. Some of the results are very useful and necessary, but many are not. For instance, expense accounts should not always need multiple approvals; people should be able to purchase approved software without going through the IT department; a pre-deal process could be established to see if deals were worth pursuing before going through all the analytics.

CAP has been successfully adapted to every type of organization - public and private, commercial and non-profit, large and small. In all of these organizations, no matter what the issue, the process remains much the same:

1. Make sure to gather the people from the organization(s) who knows the issues best.

2. Always challenge every member of the team to develop creative and applicable solutions.

3. Decide on the solutions to be adopted, as well as rejected, immediately in a public forum.

4. Empower and motivate people to carry them out as effective and timely as possible.

Leading Change: Personal Audit

Domain	What I do Well	What I Need to Work on	Score
Manage attention: To what extent do I manage: time, energy / passion, focus / agenda			
Adopt Change Roles: To What extent do I ensure that the following roles exist for change: change sponsor, change agent, change target			
Develop Personal Competence: To what extent do I demonstrate competence in: technical, personal, style			
Summary: Overall strenghts and weaknesses and evaluation			

Figure 8.5

Despite its successful impact on GE and many other organizations, CAP is not a silver-bullet, but more of a set of sound concepts, tools and best practices. When stripped to its essence, CAP allows professionals to remove some of the obstacles they encounter, so they can be more effective. In many organizations, that alone would be very significant.

The real merit of this technique is its practical approach. If your organization is struggling with the challenges of continually keeping itself lean, then CAP can help. The book mentioned above contains many inspiring worksheets, action plans, tools and hands-on case studies. Most managers today understand the value of building a learning organization. But in moving from theory into practice, managers must realize there's no one-size-fits-all strategy applicable to every company and every situation. Just be aware, however, that CAP will require a great deal of commitment and moral fortitude from leaders. Empowerment may be effective, but it is rarely comfortable for the powers that be.

Chapter 9
Using Kaizen in the Change Process

Change is not made without inconvenience, even from worse to better.

Kaizen (pronounced ki-zen) is a Japanese word constructed from two ideographs, the first of which represents change and the second goodness or virtue. Kaizen is commonly used to indicate the long-term betterment of something or someone (continuous improvement) as in the phrase "Seikatsu o kaizen suru" which means to "better one's life."

Kaizen Overview

In change management, Kaizen is used as a method that strives toward perfection by eliminating waste. It eliminates waste by empowering people with tools and a methodology for uncovering improvement opportunities and making change. Kaizen understands waste to be any activity that is not value-adding from the perspective of the customer. By value-adding, we mean any work done right the first time that materially changes a product or service in ways for which a well-informed and reasonable customer is willing to pay.

The Toyota Production System is known for kaizen, where all line personnel are expected to stop their moving production line in case of any abnormality, and suggestions for improvement are rewarded. Masaaki Imai made the term famous in his book, *Kaizen: The Key to Japan's Competitive Success.*

In my change management consulting practice at MGCG I tend to use Kaizen as a process of change, implemented as an ever-increasing and gradual practice to promote process improvements over time. This methodology suits organizations well because change is introduced slowly but consistently, a little bit at a time, step by step, thus minimizing resistance and allowing the organization to realize the small benefits resulting from their changes. This in turn motivates the organization to continue to move forward in their change process. In Kaizen, improvement is realized and maintained with a certain degree of stability and without slackening back to the previous condition. In my consulting work at companies such as International Paper and PPL Montana, Kaizen provided the conditions to make gradual process changes progress over time throughout the organization at several levels.

To understand the benefits of Kaizen better, consider that every business or corporation may need to undergo radical change, at times with higher degree, which is hard to do with any resistance, in order to survive the competition in this fast changing world. This is not in line, however, with the typical premise in the U.S. of "why-fix-it-if-it-ain't-broke philosophy." In Kaizen, its premise extends a more proactive philosophical view, where "Everything— even if it ain't broke— can be made better!"

As this book has demonstrated, no organization in the world, in any industry, can operate in an environment devoid of progressive change. Change cannot operate without a process to manage change. In Kaizen, the Wheel-of-Change is employed to drive the Kaizen process at all levels. Once this is in place, the speed-of-change must be sustained and moved upward to a level to enable the organization to cope with the external entropic influences that are always acting to break down the organization to its non-competitive level, as Figure 9.1 depicts.

Figure 9.1 – Kaizen: Continuous Improvement Balanced by Competitive Principles

In business applications, Kaizen covers most of the modules of successful Japanese concepts. Kanban, 5S, quality circles (QCs), just-in-time (JIT) delivery, automation, suggestion systems, etc., are all embedded into the Kaizen system of modern business management. Setting the structure for Kaizen is very important. This includes appointing self-directed teams that manage to:

- Analyze problems; and

- Generate solutions

Every team needs the authority to implement any necessary change when it is needed. The involvement of everyone in the team is also a must. It is typical to find in the United States, an alternative to the Kaizen approach, which is called the Kaizen Blitz (or Kaizen Event), where self-directed teams are forced to analyze problems hastily and generate curative solutions— but are immediately dissolved once the problem is solved.

In Kaizen, the setting of doable and replicable standards is imperative before those standards can be continually improved— because persistent improvements are crucial for long-term profits. In spite of distinct systemic modules, it is important to understand that Kaizen is not really a method or technique. As a system, all existing and standard programs and techniques in Kaizen are still actively used, albeit on an improved level.

Kaizen, therefore, is a lot more than incentives and rewards. It involves the support given to front-liners to help the improvement in the way work is done. Kaizen is also an important part of Total Productive Manufacturing (TPM), World-Class Manufacturing (WCM), Lean Manufacturing and Six Sigma.

Figure 9.1

97

Kaizen, therefore, can be very effective in eliminating waste by enabling workers to uncover improvement opportunities and then suggest or make changes to the process. Kaizen may also refer to different types of improvement activities. In Japan, many use the term to refer to a process that gathers suggestions for improvements from employees, while others use the practice to refer to periodic brainstorm sessions designed to improve ideas, and then select and make improvements (as in Quality Circles). In addition, some practitioners use the term to refer to special events (up to five days in length) where team members systematically detect and eliminate wasteful procedure or task in a targeted work process. Figure 9.2 illustrates a 15-step recommendation for successful Kaizen events.

Figure 9.2 - Kaizen Event Steps Outline

In our practice at MGCG, we first implement what is called *Restoration Kaizen*, which is necessary to bring the condition back to normal. This is used when an organization is in crisis and disarray. Before we can promote process improvement we need to stabilize the process, much like the work of paramedics. We can then begin using other kaizen methodologies, such as *Core Task Kaizen, Maintenance Kaizen, Improvement Kaizen* and *Innovation Kaizen.*

Kaizen is not the prerogative of management. On the contrary, it is the joint effort of both management and the workforce that brings about the growth of Kaizen activities. Kaizen activities, therefore, when it permeates throughout the whole organization, can have a significant impact on the bottom-line and the return on investment (ROI) of any business. Organizations can be assured of a high degree of sustaining power to motivate the workforce into a creative spirit for driving change.

Understanding the Basic Concepts of Total Productive Manufacturing

Total Productive Manufacturing (TPM) is a manufacturing-led program that promotes a collaborative approach among all stakeholders within an organization, particularly between operations and maintenance, in an effort to achieve production efficiency, uninterrupted operations, while ensuring a quick and proactive maintenance response to prevent equipment-specific problems. Figure 9.3 depicts the pillars of TPM.

Figure 9.3 – Pillars of TPM

TPM was introduced to achieve several objectives, but mainly to:

- Avoid wastage in a quickly changing economic environment.

Kaizen Event Steps Outline

Kaizen means "change for the good." The target of Kaizen is cost reduction by eliminating waste.

Step #0 - Event Preparation – Select event area, team, and creat team package.

Step #1 - Define the Scope and Goals of the Event

Step #2 - Train the Team. Review the World Class Tool(s) and techniques that Support the Team's Goal

Step #3 - Walk the Event Area, Observe Physical layout, Review Videos if Available. This step starts the idea creation process

Step #4 - Collect data on Event area (Scrap, Production, Time Studies, Videos, Etc.) – Develop/obtain the baseline performance measurements

Step #5 - Brainstorm Ideas – Thinking outside the box and piggybacking important here

Step #6 - Use Multi-Voting to Prioritize Top 8-10 Ideas that will be Worked on Immediately

Step #7 - Form Sub-Teams to Go Out and Try/ Implement Ideas

Figure 9.2

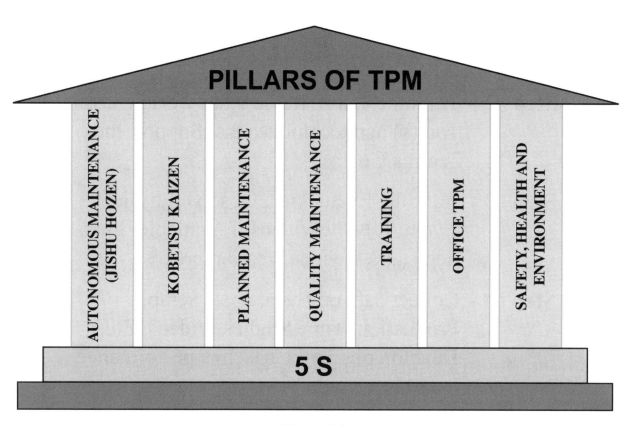

Figure 9.3

- Ensure that goods sent to customers be non-defective.

- Produce a low-batch quantity at the earliest possible time.

- Produce goods without reducing product quality.

- Reduce cost.

The goal of TPM, as illustrated in Figure 9.4, is to create a production environment that is free from mechanical breakdowns, technical disturbances, and the involvement of everyone in maintenance duties, without relying heavily on mechanics, or engineers. The modernization, along with the ongoing automation in different industries has noticeably amplified the gap between operators and their machines.

Figure 9.4 – The Goal of TPM

Several years ago, machine operators used to be limited to manning their respective work areas and posts. Every time there was a mechanical problem, operators would stop working and call in mechanics to fix the problem. Even with just the slightest hitch, operators would tend to leave the problem to be solved by the so-called "experts," for fear of aggravating the problem. In addition, the mindset was that no one wanted to do the mechanics' jobs.

By the same token, traditional mechanics were always looking for breakdowns, as they realized how indispensable specialists they have become, which assured them a stable job with lots of opportunities to fix a problem. This vicious cycle was very prevalent for several years, generating a tremendous amount of waste in various levels, from man hours and production time, all the way to opportunities lost and ballooning maintenance expense.

By adopting and adapting TPM to the process, the vicious cycle began to diminish and really come to an end. Nowadays, TPM relies on the classical Japanese concepts of autonomous maintenance, with a process mapping for cross-functional duties. There are several benefits brought by TPM. Below is a list of the main ones I have observed, which includes, but is not limited to:

- Accidents reduced to zero

- All tools in the correct place and available

- Cleaner, tidier working environment

- Defects reduced by up to 30 times

- Enhanced team working and skill building

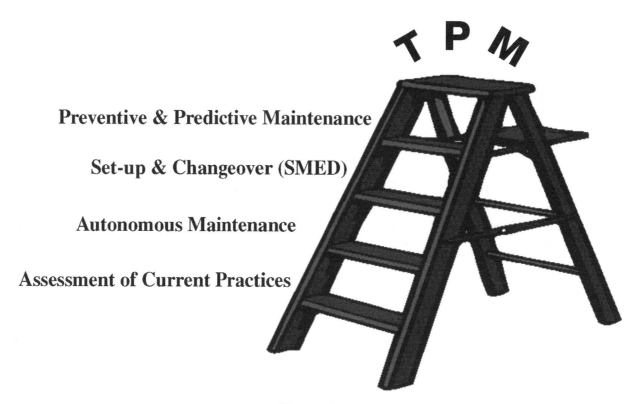

Preventive & Predictive Maintenance

Set-up & Changeover (SMED)

Autonomous Maintenance

Assessment of Current Practices

Figure 9.4

- Improvements in reliability and maintainability

- Machine breakdowns reduced by 50%

Coupled with the right tools and training, TPM can equip operators with the necessary skillset to address mechanical or equipment-related issues. Calling the engineers and mechanics is no longer necessary since operators are already prepared and confident in dealing with the problems. Autonomous maintenance by operators, therefore, is most important in TPM.

Moreover, I recommend that you offer some sort of training to all stakeholders to improve the interaction between people, operations and maintenance. At MGCG we have delivered several training programs in the U.S. and abroad, to companies such as Covanta Power Lines of the Philippines, Petrobras and International Paper of Brazil, TXU, We Energies and PPL of United States, and in all of them, the involvement of stakeholders brought homogeneous process improvement to business processes.

The incorporation of TPM in a plant involves the following elements:

- Practice of Planned Maintenance

- Improvement of Overall Equipment Effectiveness (OEE)

- Initialization of Small Group Activity (SGA)

- Early Equipment Maintenance

- Training

Undoubtedly, TPM is one of the most effective ways to create a lean organization with reduced cycle time and improved operational efficiency. The Overall Equipment Efficiency (OEE) indicator determines your production efficiency based on a given production plan. TPM makes it easier for you to improve your OEE ratio by providing a formula to quantify these losses and giving priority to the most important ones. TPM provides models and tools to achieve both short and long-term developments.

Don't Confuse TPM with TQM

The TPM program closely resembles the popular Total Quality Management (TQM) program. Many of the tools, such as employee empowerment, benchmarking, documentation, etc. used in TQM are used to implement and optimize TPM. Following are the similarities between the two.

- Total commitment to the program by upper level management is required

- Employees must be empowered to initiate corrective action, and

- A long-range outlook must be accepted, as both TPM and TQM may take a year or more to implement and is an ongoing process. Changes in employee mind-set toward job responsibilities must take place as well.

The *differences* between TQM and TPM are summarized below.

Category	TQM	TPM
Object	Quality (output and effects)	Equipment (input and cause)
Mains of attaining goal	Systematize the management; it is software-oriented	Employee participation; it is hardware-oriented
Target	Quality for PPM	Elimination of losses and waste

Understanding the Basic Concepts of World-Class Manufacturing

The motivating factor behind the World Class Manufacturing (WCM) initiative is two-pronged: first, it puts into action operations management improvements, across all functional units, departments or sectors, and second, to equip organizations with tool that will enable them to become competitive and responsive in a ever changing market landscape.

WCM is a process that integrates cross-functional operations in a way that meets exactly what customers specifically need and want from a product. WCM, however, is not an end in itself, but a definitive process. As a process, organizations are likely to achieve much better results associated with successful implementation of industry-tested methods.

For several years, manufacturing has always focused in its internal operations and was very compartmentalized. Workers tend to complete their jobs without a good understanding, if any, of the impact of their work on the whole operation, and if their contribution had any important impact on customers and final products.

Threfore, critical functions such as quality control, engineering, purchasing, and other similar tasks, were clearly separated and often described as a "wall approach" to manufacturing. These so-called "silos" inhibited direct and consistent interaction between the many cross-functions, while also isolating decision makers from both, the inside and outside business environments.

As a result of this isolation, products tend not to meet customer expectations, while internal operational snags, such as losses in time, money, opportunity, and so on typically proliferated.

The goal of implementing a lean word-class enterprise is to improve all aspects of business, to capitalize on the advances gained from applying technically proven trade methods and principles in order to be profitable, and, eventually, to be globally competitive.

As the manufacturing sector faces new challenges in the midst of competition, WCM advocates strive continuously to improve on the areas of delivery, safety, quality, operating cost and profit margins simultaneously, eliminating waste in the production system by applying appropriate tools and techniques at all levels within the organization. By examining their strengths and weaknesses, manufacturing organizations are taking positive steps to respond to the challenges of becoming world-class competitors.

Understanding the Basic Concepts of Lean Manufacturing

Inspired by Kaizen, lean manufacturing is a management philosophy that focus on the elimination of waste in the production systems. In other words, as depicted in Figure 9.5, it's like getting rid of unnecessary "fats" and waste in the workplace that provide no added value to a product. The ultimate goal of this methodology is to improve and speed up production by eliminating quantifiable waste as far as manufacturing/production is concerned. Therefore, when we speak of Lean Manufacturing, it means addressing "non-productive resources" in key areas of operations that are not beneficial to the entire production process.

Figure 9.5 – Lean manufacturing can eliminate the fat and waste of business and industrial processes

In simplest terms, the lean manufacturing approach directly identifies common problems in operations— like defective equipment, overproduction, loose inventories, time-motion lags, over-processing, over staffing, delivery issues, unreasonable floor space, surplus and material leftovers, quality losses, etc.— and immediately addresses and corrects these with the definitive purpose of reducing lead-times, improving quality, lowering production costs, and achieving substantial results.

Lean manufacturing can help you reduce labor costs, minimize inventory and improve quality by implementing lean practices and thinking. Lean techniques can be applied to non-manufacturing as well as manufacturing environments. By eliminating waste, minimizing production disruptions and increasing the predictability of business processes, lean manufacturing can tremendously impact the bottom line of any organization. Below is a 7-Step improvement plan I tend to recommend:

1. Discuss and better understand the current process.

2. Map the current process in detail.

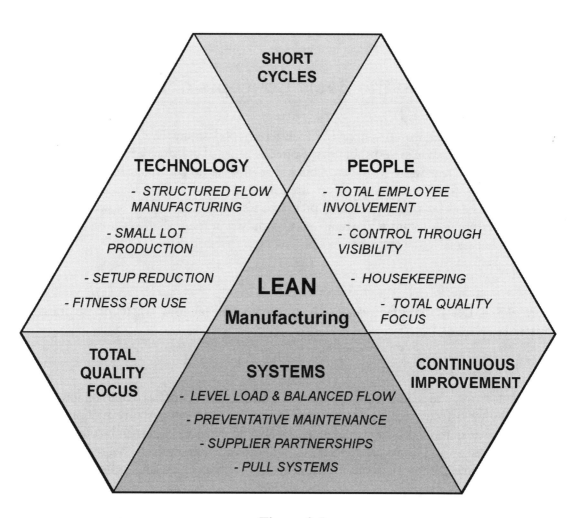

SHORT CYCLES

TECHNOLOGY
- STRUCTURED FLOW MANUFACTURING
- SMALL LOT PRODUCTION
- SETUP REDUCTION
- FITNESS FOR USE

PEOPLE
- TOTAL EMPLOYEE INVOLVEMENT
- CONTROL THROUGH VISIBILITY
- HOUSEKEEPING
- TOTAL QUALITY FOCUS

LEAN Manufacturing

TOTAL QUALITY FOCUS

SYSTEMS
- LEVEL LOAD & BALANCED FLOW
- PREVENTATIVE MAINTENANCE
- SUPPLIER PARTNERSHIPS
- PULL SYSTEMS

CONTINUOUS IMPROVEMENT

Figure 9.5

106

3. Educate team on best-in-class processes.

4. Have the team identify opportunities.

5. Map out the new processes

6. Develop a detailed implementation plan.

7. Support implementation.

Putting in place a lean manufacturing system offers tangible and measurable results in terms of quality, efficiency and output. A rationalized operating expense strengthens one's competitive edge; improving production processes suggests better functionality; enhanced functionality means better quality; better quality means larger market demand; more demand requires increased output; and more output means higher sales revenues.

Lean manufacturing is not only a project or program. It is a way of thinking. The implementation of lean manufacturing encompasses the following stages, as illustrated in Figure 9.6:

- Data Collection Stage

- Data Analysis and Development of Solution Stage

- Implementation Stage

Figure 9.6 – Lean Manufacturing Implementation Phases

During the Data Collection Stage the following activities relating to lean manufacturing are performed:

- Time and Motion Studies

- Establishment or review of Process Flow Charts

- Investigating product families

- Investigating bottle necks and problem areas

Data collection is comprised of information gathered on the current state of facilities and operations. The output will be a document detailing the current state of facilities and operations, as relevant for lean manufacturing.

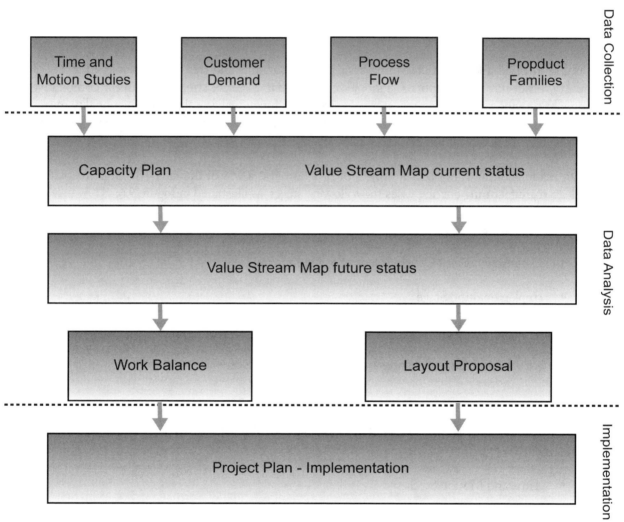

Figuer 9.6

During the Data Analysis Stage the following activities relating to lean manufacturing are performed:

- Establishment of a Capacity Plan

- Determination of the current state of the Value Stream Map

- Value Stream Map future state – micro and macro levels

- Determining the Work Balance

- Design of a Layout Proposal

- Preparation of a Project Implementation Plan

This stage will have three documents as output:

- An Evaluation Document comprising analysis and calculation

- A Design Document proposing a solution leading to a

- Project Implementation Plan

During the Implementation Stage the following activities relating to lean manufacturing are performed:

- Execution of the Project Implementation Plan.

- Design and manufacture of special tools and material handling equipment

- Outsourcing of Capex (if needed)

- Training of relevant staff

Lean Manufacturing techniques are not limited to the manufacturing sector (i.e., factories, production, assembly lines, etc.). As a matter of fact, they can also be applied to service-oriented industries, the government bureaucracy, or even at home or in the office, because these work places have elements that do not provide value to the whole work process. These elements, which are appropriately identified and analyzed, are nothing but "waste" that needs to be eliminated.

Understanding the Basic Concepts of Six Sigma

Developed by Motorola in 1987, Six Sigma (6Σ) is a business strategy and management concept that sets the highest standard of discipline in meeting extremely high objectives, including the collection of data and analyzes of results to achieve an almost zero-degree of error tolerance, as a strategy to reduce waste, defects and irregularities in both products and services. The Greek letter sigma (Σ) is used to statistically signify the disparity from a given standard.

When Motorola introduced the Six Sigma, the scheme was at first applied to repetitive manufacturing processes. Today it has evolved into a constant and broad structured process of improving all aspects of operation to consistently meet customer satisfaction in both products and services, as Six Sigma is driven by the dictates of consumers.

The Motorola approach encourages leanness, simplicity and the correct attitude of "doing-it-right-the-first-time." Six Sigma proponents claim that they have achieved 50% process cost reduction, improved cycle-time, reduced wastage and increased customer satisfaction, all while maintaining production quality.

In statistical parlance, Six Sigma is the "nickname" of six standard deviations from the mean—which numerically translates to about two (2) defects per billion. In layman's language, a particular manufacturing process cannot go beyond producing two (2) defects per billion parts produced. Six Sigma is, therefore, achieved only if defects are kept to an almost perfect production rate, equivalent to 99.9997%. In other words, the widely used failure rate of 3.4 parts per million, which corresponds to roughly 4.5 sigmas, is already an unacceptable mathematical figure.

Since Six Sigma focuses on process quality, it is imperative to measure how many defects are in a process and thereby figure out how to systematically eliminate errors, adopt fine-tuning methods, and achieve concrete and measurable results which are as close to being perfect as possible. Once the level of Six Sigma excellence and consistency is realized, quality control normally is no longer necessary.

The 6-Sigma Characteristic

Six Sigma is a meticulous, precise and calculated analytical process for anticipating and addressing quality improvement. It is likewise an essential yardstick in solving process-related problems. It can also be applied to a gamut of strategies, tools, formulas and methodologies to improve the profitability of companies through defect reduction, yield improvement, improved consumer satisfaction and optimum product performance.

A Word about the *Belts*

The Six Sigma is implemented using trained key players known as "Black Belts," "Green Belts" and "Master Black Belt". The "Green Belt" is a person trained in Six Sigma methodology who is a member of the Six Sigma process improvement action team. A "Black Belt," on the other hand, is a person who is part of the leadership structure for process improvement teams. These *belters* are technically oriented personnel who are highly regarded to lead teams and advise management-level officers. The "Master Black Belt" acts as the program manager or Six Sigma director. He checks and watches over process improvement projects and provides support to Black Belts, as needed. A Master Black Belt teaches other Six Sigma students and helps them achieve Green and Black belt status.

In Six Sigma, statistical tools usually follow the DMAIC (Define, Measure, Analyze, Implement and Control) steps, as depicted in Figure 9.7. Specific tools are used as control charts covering Pareto diagrams, process mapping, and value stream mapping and scatter plots. In addition, Lean Manufacturing and TPM tools are used, as well as Kaizen, 5S, OEE and LCC.

Figure 9.7 - Six Sigma statistical tools usually follow the DMAIC steps

The Six Sigma way is to understand the customers' needs, gather valuable information and data from the processes, and make accurate statistical analysis from it to improve the processes. At the end of the day, making it to the Six Sigma level is learning from the mistakes and successful process deployments in the past, and getting the required support from co-workers and the valuable backing of top management.

If companies are able to make Six Sigma take place in their respective backyards, quality control becomes an unnecessary preoccupation— and companies will definitely have a happy, satisfied and growing customer base.

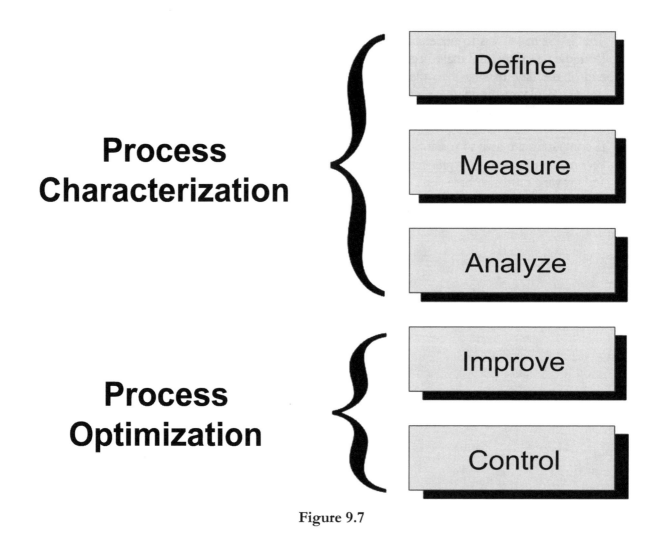

Figure 9.7

Chapter 10
Becoming a Learning Organization: Ready to Change

Like chameleons, companies must adapt and learn to strive in their environment very quickly.

"What is the big deal about change management?" you might ask. I wouldn't argue that the movement is getting a bit long in the tooth. The number of change management conferences is down, even though I have been presenting papers on knowledge and change management almost three times a year. And I am still waiting for *People Magazine* to stop being stubborn and name a CM experts as one of its "25 Most Intriguing People of the Year."

Change management may be quiet, buried under knowledge management best practice in many cases, but it is not dead. As chapters one and two pointed out, CM is just beginning to penetrate the fabric of many businesses, and statistics alone prove it. The problem is that the early, flashy-but-insubstantial applications, such as best practices and lessons learned, for example, have given way to broadly focused initiatives that are transforming the way organizations work, particularly in government circles and Fortune 100 corporations. Any change takes time, and for the most part, it is never amenable to shallow, sensationalistic journalistic treatment. In fact, only the most profound, gifted analysts and writers can comprehend and express it.

The value of organizational learning should be recognized, as change management can easily be seen as a key corporate asset that must be leveraged and exploited for competitive purpose. In this emerging, globalized and rapidly changing market, creative ideas and innovative thinking are essential. Many organizations, at least in theory, have been trying to become a learning organization. However, the effort has not been as practical as it should be, and best practices are not easily found. This chapter attempts to provide you with a roadmap to turn your company into a learning one, with practical examples that you can apply the next day. This chapter also helps you shape yourself with the attributes required to successfully meet and fulfill this challenge. After reading this chapter, I strongly suggest you add another layer of knowledge about learning organizations by reading Bob Garratt's book, *The Learning Organization: Developing Democracy at*

Work.[1] This book will arm you with all the "how-tos" (now that you have the "know-how") of turning an enterprise into a learning one, and living to talk about it.

Building a Learning Organization

How do you know if you have a learning organization? What are the clues you should look for in defining it? In building and maintaining a learning organization you must look for traits that define the organization, nurture some of them, and eliminate others, so you can bridge the knowledge gap in the organization to allow a successful knowledge transfer into action (from know-how to how-to). But what are the traits that should be nurtured, and what about those that should be eliminated? Such a task is near impossible, unless you have a clear agenda of what a learning organization means to your organization. You must have a very-well defined learning agenda.

Having a Defined Learning Agenda

Any learning organization should have a defined learning agenda. Does yours have one? Does your organization have a clear picture of the knowledge requirements it needs to strive and be successful? Look for these attitudes:

- Does your organization know what it needs to know, regardless of the subject, be it competition, market capitalization, technology trends, customer profiling and services, production processes, knowledge collaboration and information gathering, etc.?

- Is your organization pursuing these knowledge goals with multiple approaches? Once your organization is able to identify its needs for knowledge, it must pursue it with several approaches, which should not be reduced to training and education alone. It should include experimental approaches, research studies via analyst firms or in-house resources, simulations, customer surveys, benchmarking when appropriate, etc.

Being Open to Dissonant Information

Learning organizations should be open to dissonant information. To bridge the knowledge gap that stops organizations from acting on what they know, or need to know, learning organizations must become simultaneously effective and efficient in their actions. However, this requires a higher level of continuous learning between the leaders who drives the organization, including CKOs and not just CEOs, the staff delivering the organization's products or service, and the costumers of this organization. You must look at your organization as a complex adaptive human system trying to become a generative system, more than just mindless machines or merely structured systems. A learning organization is one that breathes and lives out of paradox, of dissonant information, so learn not to shoot the messengers who bring bad news or raise paradoxical ideas! Your goal is to help the organization flourish in such an environment, as a

---

[1] HarperCollins Publishers, UK, 2001

child does in its early stages of life. Be prepared to believe, strive and guide your organization in doing the same when facing paradoxes such as these:

- You may be losing when wining – When your product is a success, or your processes are working, the tendency is to let it be, not to fix what is not broken. However, if you look back to all the success stories, those businesses that failed to respond to a new challenge disappeared or were replaced. The American automobile industry went through it with the Japanese. Apple Computers committed the same mistake with their Apple and Macintosh lines of computers in the past. What happened to excellent software applications such as WordPerfect, dBase II, III and IV, Lotus SmartSuite? What happened to Netscape, or better yet Mosaic, Compaq, Digital Equipment Corp.? Organizations, and their products, will die if they can't keep up with the rate of change in their industry, and trying to play the new game with the old rules is a recipe for disaster. I've seen several organizations not being able to make sense of pseudo-chaotic information and feedback coming in from a tumultuous global market, and trying to react with obsolete tactics, just to waste capital, people and time, and eventually the eagerness to fight on. That's when you realize that in today's business, learning organizations must compete and cooperate with their competitors. The "either or" solutions no longer will hold, except for when we either compete successfully or die. I recommend a great book entitled "Co-opetition," by Brandenberger & Nalebuff, for excellent discussion and knowledge on co-opetition. [2]

- Choices as cause – If your company is not adopting generative learning, which is discussed in more details later on in this chapter, then you are relying on adaptive learning systems. Such systems always show patterns that can never be predicted in advance, regardless of the familiarity you have with the inputs. This is because you are relying on a reactive system. Thus the outcomes are the result of mere random choices made by members of the staff or organization. Choice here is synonymous with chance, and chance is the one driving the outcome! How about that for a managerial style? I hope you will find it as disturbing as I did when I finally accepted this paradox.

- Being reasonable can be limiting – In today's business front, being rational is not necessarily being business savvy. Actually, most entrepreneurs I know or read about use a great amount of intuition in their everyday business decisions. Leaders with tremendous business acumen often feel the advantages that their structural positioning in the business network offers them, and learn how to exploit the stream of opportunities that their position allows to flow in their direction. A key factor here is that professionals must learn to identify these opportunities, and use intuition in association with the structures surrounding the business and themselves. For too many CEOs and other senior staff, to rely on intuition and feelings, and to try to tie these insights to business structures, is too intimidating, to say the least. Most executives are too set in their ways as convergent-thinking, data-rational, reductionist managers to accept such a paradoxical management challenge. That's why every business plan has a provision for an exit strategy, which I call the moment when the ostrich puts its head in the sand, and not even know where the kick came from. Instead, I advocate a more Hellenic posture to business, armed with a

---

[2] HarperCollins Business, 1995

breast plate but totally unprotected back, just in case I feel tempted to give my back to business challenges.

- Organizations are not simply structures – Organizations are much more than simple structures, as they suffer the influence of human process energies, both negative and positive. People are the ones driving the organization. If people are energized, the organization will be energized.

To change the behavior of such organizations is a very difficult task, and many give up in the process. Actually that's one of the main reasons the big six consulting firms keep on returning to the same organizations over and over, and telling them through reports and best practices the same things, which basically challenges their status quo and calls for changes in those areas. A true learning organization will not avoid discussing sensitive issues and making necessary changes in areas such as dissention of ranks, unhappy customers, preemptive moves by the competition, and issues with disruptive and new technologies. Typically, information gathered in these areas is filtered and there is a resistance to deal with it, especially at the senior level, where people tend to avoid being confronted with ideas that may change their status quo or require them to change or leave their comfort zone.

Avoiding Repeated Mistakes: Surviving Business Darwinism

Certainly it would be very hard to find a business professional that would also be an adept to Darwin's theory of the origin of species. But much can be learned from Darwin's theory and strategically applied to learning organizations today. Just as in the theory of evolution, in business only the fittest survive.

As organizations virtualize themselves to reach across borders on a global market perspective, the Web has become a business world in which companies (or species) must constantly adapt to their changing business environment or face extinction. The Web has become a world in which business must continue to grow in a profitable direction, and develop new skills and traits, or perish.

For learning organizations, doing business on the Web requires companies (or digital life-forms) to instinctively know with whom to cooperate and with whom to compete. All this takes place in an environment where the business conditions (or life) can suddenly and drastically change, for better or for worse. More than ever, mistakes can be deadly. As Darwin commented, surviving in this complex web of relations is a tough task. So it is for a company to survive and conduct business on the Web.

Strong market forces in the increasingly competitive Web economy are forcing companies to develop new strategies for economic survival. As the Web traverses its especially frenetic evolution, it also gives birth to an entirely new breed of start-up companies and enterprises that could not have existed in a traditional economy. Further, these new companies are forcing older corporate models to evolve in new ways, reengineering themselves and producing new business models necessary for their own survival.

116

E-business is becoming a fierce battle, and rivals are clawing their market share by developing new business models and inventing breakthrough business tactics especially suited to their swiftly shifting surroundings. As with chameleons, in e-business companies must adapt and learn to strive in their environment very quickly. Thus learning organizations must learn from their mistakes and past experiences, share the knowledge internally, and ensure that errors are not repeated elsewhere.

It is possible to turn a failure into a success, a weakness into strength. A productive failure is the one that capitalizes on the lessons learned to lead to insights, understanding and innovation. The key to preventing repeated mistakes is to accept when one is committed the first time, and repent from it. Learning organizations will draw their strength from their weaknesses, as it is not the success they remember the most, but the mistakes they learned from, and which allowed them to achieve success.

The resistance in dealing with the knowledge gap, in remaining an adaptive learning organization will be responsible for several business failures. The proof of it is the dotcom phenomenon. This scenario is only going to get worse and companies embracing e-business must realize it. At first the Web was an unformed mass of perky expressions and corporate brochures, as early users somewhat feared the technology. But then fear gave way to experimentation and successful experimentation gave way to confidence. Now confidence is inspiring users to trust the Web, and do business in it, faithfully. This faith is leading to mass acceptance, generating the biggest market place ever known.

This new trend is pushing the world's biggest companies to gaze toward a future in which much, if not most, of their purchasing, invoicing, document exchange, and logistics are transferred from stand-alone computer networks connected by people, paper and phone calls, to a seamless Web that spans the globe and connects more than a billion computing devices.

Therefore, I strongly believe online business-to-business (B2B) will explode at an unprecedented rate, becoming the centerpiece of a mind-boggling multi-trillion-dollar Web economy. Worldwide shipments of e-procurement solutions (ePS) software, for example, will grow to almost 10 times their present size, from $243 million in 1999 to almost $5.2 billion by the end of 2007, with a Cumulative Average Growth Rate (CAGR) of nearly 55 percent[3].

Organizations that resist such a trend or attempt to adapt to it later on in the game will do so at their on peril. By eliminating the tedious paper-based procurement process, buying organizations are saving money previously allocated to the many resources needed to complete these processes. ePS not only reduces costs by simplifying order processing, but also by drastically cutting or eliminating maverick spending, and providing access to marketplaces and trading communities that feature supplier products at competitive prices.

Danger Lurks Beneath

Beware that even though the Web economy is thriving, adaptive learning organizations engaged in e-business must watch the danger lurking beneath. On the Web everything is possible, so don't

---

[3] , According to the ARC's E-Procurement Solutions (ePS) Worldwide Outlook (1999).

be surprised when some of today's most dominant e-businesses (or creatures) are rendered helpless in the face of rapid, unforeseen change. As dotcoms fight over their share of the Internet market, competition gets more and more barbarous, giving room to rapid consolidations and hostile takeovers.

I believe these early skirmishes are only the tip of the iceberg of what is to come. There are lots of companies on the Web, but not many businesses. Unless organizations become learning organizations, and carefully plan their e-business strategies and monitor them constantly, they will end up being victims of natural e-business Darwinism. I strongly believe most organizations will resist this concept, as they resist the value of CKOs and knowledge management. Thus there will be super-consolidations on the e-business horizon with very few winners. After all, who needs thousands of bookstores or drugstores on the Web?

Learning organizations should not only be concerned with low prices, but with branding and efficient inventory and distribution systems that enable them to better manage their total cost of ownership (TCO) and substantially increase their return of investment (ROI).

In helping learning organizations to better position, manage and compete in e-business, integration applications are a must, and CKOs and business leaders must capitalize on that opportunity. For instance, take the e-procurement trend. There is no doubt that in B2B situations e-procurement is the killer application for commercial use of the Internet. Given the number of benefits these applications offer businesses, organizations may not survive if they do not invest in them. E-procurement solutions simplify e-business transactions between companies, making this kind of application crucial to the success of B2B e-business.

As for business-to-consumer (B2C) e-commerce, we have another major challenge for learning organizations. Web sites require excellent sales support to attract customers and be successful. Ordinary database and full text queries, as well as simple profiles, do not provide the expected level of service. Knowledge technologies can fuel intelligent searching, personalized feedback dialogs and sophisticated knowledge navigation, which provide customers with the kind of help and comfort they look for. The results are higher traffic and turnover, and increased customer satisfaction.

Therefore e-commerce Web sites have to provide easy to use interfaces to attract customers. The number of clicks to place the product in the shopping cart has to be as small as possible, and additional information about related products has to tempt customer to buy more. Both requirements can be somehow fulfilled by traditional database applications and search techniques, but knowledge technologies can fuel e-commerce applications. Case studies show that e-commerce sites powered by knowledge technologies can drastically increase traffic, customer satisfaction, and shop turnover.

Preserving Critical Knowledge

Is your organization prepared to lose a talented professional? What would your organization do if critical skills were to disappear with the departure of a key professional? In other words, is your company prepared to lose critical tacit knowledge?

118

Explicit knowledge can always be captured by knowledge technology solutions, KM implementations and knowledge databases. But tacit, unarticulated and, worse, unshared knowledge locked in the head of single professional can be devastating to a business. Learning organizations can avoid such problems by institutionalizing essential knowledge. This requires senior management to codify this knowledge in policies and procedures, retain it in reports and e-mails, and disperse it through brownbags and other forms of organizational gatherings. To avoid losing valuable knowledge, learning companies turn knowledge into a common property, instead of a providence of individuals or small groups.

Acting on What the Organization Knows

The definition of success is vision in action. Thus for learning organizations to be successful they must turn their vision into action. Action without a vision is like sailing uncharted waters without a compass. By the same token, vision without action is just an idea, a dream. Learning organizations should not be only a repository of knowledge. For that, let the Universities and business schools do their job.

Learning organizations make sure to act on what they know by taking advantage of new learning and by adapting their behaviors accordingly. If organizations don't use the information they have worked so hard to acquire, what good is it? What good is it if an organization realizes an untapped market but fails to take advantage of it?

Therefore it is very important that a learning organization is aware of what knowledge is, how to identify and capture it, and transfer it across the organization, effectively turning it into action. Otherwise the organization will never grow or succeed.

Learning Agenda

The first step in becoming a learning organization is to have a learning agenda. Otherwise, what you have is an adaptive organization, bowing with the winds of business, rolling with the punches of the competition.

If your organization has a learning agenda, as discussed earlier in this chapter, then it will be ready to move on to the next stage, being open for conflicts.

Open to Conflicts

At this stage, the learning organization will face a lot of conflicts, as it will be faced with different and individual agendas from several senior staff members, and the organization as a whole. To avoid these conflicts can be fatal for the organization. If anything, the conflicts will bring the organization back to its first stage, where a learning agenda needs to be redefined or truly established. However, if the organization is open to conflicts, it can then deal with the acceptable differences, goals and mission statements, and get a unified set of goals for the company as a whole. Once senior staff and the remaining organization are unified in the understanding of what they are, where they are and where they want to go, as well as what it will take to get them there, then the organization is ready to move to the next step, which is avoiding mistakes.

Avoiding Mistakes

This is an equally important stage. At this point, the learning organization should have a well-defined learning agenda, which means it should know where it needs to go and have a plan to get there. The organization should also have purged the demons afflicting its goals, resolved any conflicts it had with members of the team, and implemented strategies to achieve such goals.

Now it is time to avoid the mistakes of the past, and learn from current mistakes so as to avoid them in the future. Failure in doing so will inevitably bring the organization back to the previous step, being open to conflict. Invariably this is the cause for recurring mistakes, either because they were not dealt with in the past or because there was a conflict avoidance when dealing with them, which prevented the organization of learning from it. Beware that once an organization steps back into a previous stage, the lack of moment and increased inertia tends to bring the organization all the way back to the eye of the knowledge gap tornado.

Therefore at this stage the organization must be very keen in avoiding repeated mistakes and concentrate on getting ready, shielded from potential loss of knowledge, in the case of losing a key professional or group.

Preventing the Loss of Knowledge

At this stage, the learning organization has shifted from an adaptive learning to a generative learning mode. It is now thinking proactively instead of reactively. The goal here is to proactively shield itself from loss of knowledge, which would bring the organization back to a repeated mistake, a previous stage.

At this point an organization should not only be ready to prevent the loss of knowledge but also to turn learn into action.

Turning Learning into Action

This is the final stage of the knowledge gap tornado, before the organization starts the process again, now in a outer ring around the tornado. If successful, the learning organization will be able to not only turn learning into action, which will tangibly and measurable impact the organization and the business bottom-line, but the company will also receive a sort of reward by acquiring silos of knowledge, developed during its growth and transformation into a learning organization.

These silos of information are very important in fueling the next cycle of growth of the company, making it knowledgeably stronger, more competitive and united in all fronts. At this stage the company breaks free from the stronger centrifugal forces of the tornado, as it distances itself from the eye. In addition, the company has business and learning momentum in its favor.

Figure 10.1 – Turning learning into action

120

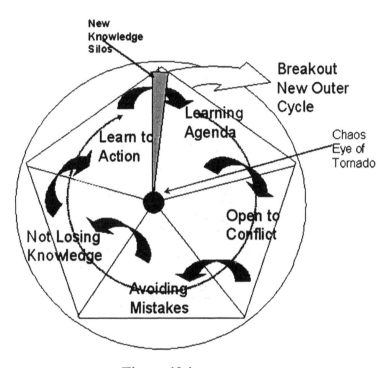

Figure 10.1

As with all the other stages, if the learning organization is not able to turn learning into action, chances are it is lacking knowledge somewhere, or it has lost knowledge in the process, either through the departure of a key professional, wherein knowledge had not been institutionalized, or by a failure in the institutionalization of knowledge within the organization.

All Things are Impermanent: Bridges Don't Last

It is evident that all things are impermanent, including the bridges used to overcome gaps. But doesn't it seem that they used to fade or change more slowly? No long ago, businesses were experiencing massive restructurings, re-engineering and redirection. Skills and tools were needed to respond to various impacts, to help us create rather than react. But now we are spinning faster, and the group change tools do not always seem to work. The reason is two-fold: mistakenly identifying problems, and believing once a gap is bridged it will always be bridged.

Both assumptions are incorrect. First, many executives have difficulty distinguishing a problem from a predicament. Problems can always be solved, while predicaments can only be coped with. Spending time and energy on a predicament will only bring frustration, discouragement and desolation. Most issues one faces in life, including marriage, family affairs, and business affairs and so on, are complicated and inescapable dilemmas; they tend to be predicaments that make not a single option a best option, where all tend to be relative. Business in the 21st century is a lot like that. In this new economy, MIS, or management of information systems, most often will not serve the executive management, either because these systems will be inadequate or because the executive will be computer naïve. Besides, how good is stored data if it is not real-time?

By accepting that all things are impermanent, executives can take advantage of business tools that helps them solve problems and accept predicaments, actually taking advantage of this knowledge, as those are very possibility the only consistent data they will have. Thus some strategies to cope with the paradox of bridging gaps are outlined below.

Know What Matters

Michael Korda[4], the novelist, once said that "the first rule of success, and the one that supersedes all others, is to have energy. It is important to know how to concentrate it and focus it on the important things, instead of frittering it away on trivia." The most powerful thing you can do at any moment is re-focus. Ask yourself: What do you want to achieve? Why is this important?

Keep in mind that gaps are inevitable; you will always have to deal with the consequences of change in the organization. And the fact that your organization is learning only makes the advent of change even more obvious, as awareness is part of the process. Once you learn that there is no face lost in abandoning all hope of completely avoiding gaps, you can much more comfortably get down to the task of managing how to decide which bits of it are worthy of your attention, and more importantly, which are not.

---

[4] In *Another Life*, Delta, 2000

Your goal should always be bridging the gap, which is the same as transcending, not adapting. Many people come to this epiphany when they have their second child. All the angst spent worrying about potential crises with the first child turns into considered risk management. With the first one it's *"Oh my Gosh - keep him away from that - it's got dirt on it!!,"* and then panic sets in. With the second one it's *"Well, it's only dirt,"* and serenity flows. Once you learn that gaps are part of business and transcending them part of the drill, you then become a knowing organization, dependent on the next gap, so you can learn one more time and set a distance from your competitors. Much like surfers, you should look at gaps as the waves, the necessary element for a fun ride, full of emotions, accomplishments and lessons learned.

The trick is to continually assess issues based on the amount of influence you have in determining their outcome. If you have no influence, your worrying isn't going to help, so don't worry. If you have a moderate amount, do what you can and be satisfied that you've done your best. If you have great influence, then set it as a priority and influence away. No time to worry.

Maintain Your Network

No organization is an island, and the 21st century will be characterized by partnerships and alliances. Any organization operates best when interdependent, not leaning but supported. It may be time to reevaluate partners, to reassess alliances, to reenergize team consciousness in the workplace and community of practices.

One of the keys to bridging gaps is the ability to tap into support facilities. Productivity almost invariably increases when it is delegated, leveraged and pulled together. Thus maintain your network of contacts:

- Begin using a contact manager

- Keep all of your contacts – business, school, friends, acquaintances

- Be a source of referrals

- Let organizations know you don't mind being referred

- Build a select distribution list of supply chain, distribution channels and partners that you want to keep posted on what you are doing

Effective Leadership Does Not Avoid Conflicts

I believe that most executives may not have a problem with this, but as Wall Street gets more and more sensitive about the financials of any organization, there are executives that waste an enormous amount of time and energy in developing and maintaining a peachy mask. Today's business environment allows no time for that! It's time for empowerment.

Some areas you should be aware of include:

- Protecting the organization's interests from unscrupulous profit-making gigs

- Protecting organizations from unscrupulous employee tax shelter schemes

- Addressing privacy issues generated by the Internet and other new technologies

- Monitoring the stewardship of the organization's assets

Learn to Live with Less

This is a strange concept for many of us in business who have spent much of our working lives running after more physical assets for the corporation. When the economy moves fast, the less baggage and overhead an organization have to carry the better; after all, everything is impermanent! Look what happened to Digital Equipment Corporation and Data General, to cite only few examples. Traveling light - in many ways - becomes more effective. KPMG is an example of such a premise. In several centers they use the hotelling system to accommodate many times the number of consultants it has in the same facility.

Choose Care over Fear

Marianne Williamson, who wrote the words Nelson Mandela used in his inaugural address, was the first to suggest the choice of care over fear. There are only two fundamental emotions - love and fear. Anything that isn't one is the other. Until recently we didn't talk about this in the corporate arena. Now we know tough love builds good teams, and gaps are exacerbated by fear. This is not about being soft and gooey - you know that. It's about finding a way to address issues head on with an intelligent mix of courage, commitment and compassion.

Gaps are inevitable. In the sense that perturbation is evolutionary, it's also desirable. But managing it is essential. It's no use for any of us to hope that someone else will do it. Do you have your own personal strategies in place?

Therefore, any executive staff, when acting in that capacity, should have two general but very important duties:

- To ensure that they have an adequate information flow regarding all the activities and affairs of the organization, especially with regard to finances

- To act solely on what they believe is in the best interest of the organization and not in the personal interest of themselves, their private business interests, or their associates, including avoiding conflicts of interest.

A Matter of Communication: Avoiding Predicaments

Richard Farson[5] encourages leaders to think "beyond the conventional wisdom...to understand how the ways we think shape what we see, and how paradox and absurdity inevitably play a part in our every action." According to him, we think we want creativity or change, but we really don't. We stifle creativity by playing intellectual games, judging and evaluating, dealing in absolutes, thinking stereotypically, and not trusting our own experiences (and training our employees not to trust theirs).

Nonetheless, although it is true that leadership is trapped by many paradoxes, communication can be an important vehicle to bridge gaps and management of gaps. Communication provides the link through which information is shared, opinions are expressed, feedback is provided and goals are formulated. Work cannot be done without communication. It is necessary to communicate in order to advise, train and inform. Members of an organization must translate corporate goals into action and results. In order for this to happen, all forms of correspondence must flow freely throughout the organizational structure.

There is also a correlation between the willingness of every level of the organization to communicate openly and frequently, and the satisfaction expressed by the workers. Most organizational predicaments, from misunderstandings to disasters, from small frustrations to major morale problems, can be traced back to either a lack of communication or ineffective technique.

Communication does not take place unless there is understanding between the communicator and the audience. Simply learning to write or read or speak is not enough. Does one make music by merely striking the keys of a piano? The difference between making noise and making music is study, understanding technique, and practice, practice, practice. The same is true for communications. The difference between talking, reading, writing or hearing, and communicating, is study, understanding technique, and practice, practice, practice.

Therefore, executive staff should examine the process of communication within the organization and strive to increase their propensity for successful communication. Messages must be clearly stated, brief and well-planned, and must answer the questions who, what, when, where and why.

The sending modes of communication are speaking, writing and nonverbal messages. The receiving modes are listening, reading and observation. Each of these modes is used in the process of getting work accomplished. Improvement in the effectiveness of any one of these modes will result in higher productivity and increased satisfaction. It is not simply a matter of how much one communicates, but how well.

Bridging the Gap from the Top Down or from the Bottom Up?

Organizational leaders are perpetually faced with a series of questions:

---

[5] In *Managing of the Absurd: Paradox in Leadership*, Touchstone Books, 1997

- In bridging a major gap (a change effort), should you drive the change or build the bridge, from the top down or the bottom up?

- How would you make sure your organization is constantly innovating and at the same time delivering a standardized level of service?

- How would you encourage your senior management group to work as a team and at the same time not lose your star performers?

Although leadership is defined above as the management of paradoxes, paradoxes are not managed in the way that problems are. Paradoxes have to be constantly managed, for they are never "solved" like problems. Additionally, paradox can be critical to integrity. If a concept is paradoxical, that itself should suggest that it smacks of integrity, which gives off the ring of truth. Conversely, if a concept is not in the least paradoxical, you should be suspicious of it and suspect that it has failed to integrate some aspect of the whole. Such a premise is very important in generating and evaluating Koulopoulos' concept of collective corporate wisdom.

It is common today for CEOs to report that "all management is people management." Given that Christianity, also, could be described as being about "people management," it is not surprising that the work world and the religious world would share the phenomenon of paradox.